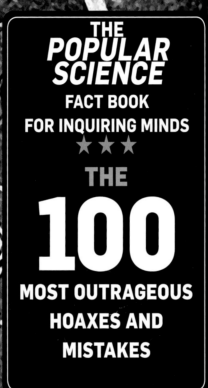

THE *POPULAR SCIENCE*

FACT BOOK
FOR INQUIRING MINDS

★ ★ ★

THE
100
MOST OUTRAGEOUS
HOAXES AND
MISTAKES

Edited by
Susan Elkin

Cavendish Square

New York

This edition published in 2018 by Cavendish Square Publishing, LLC
243 5th Avenue, Suite 136, New York, NY 10016

First Edition

Website: cavendishsq.com

This publication represents the opinions and views of the author based on his or her personal experience, knowledge, and research. The information in this book serves as a general guide only. The author and publisher have used their best efforts in preparing this book and disclaim liability rising directly or indirectly from the use and application of this book.

All websites were available and accurate when this book was sent to press.

Cataloging-in-Publication Data

Names: Elkin, Susan/ editor.
Title: The 100 most outrageous hoaxes and mistakes / Susan Elkin.
Description: New York : Cavendish Square, 2018. | Series: The popular science fact book for inquiring minds| Includes bibliographical references and index.
Identifiers: ISBN 9781502632890 (library bound)
Subjects: LCSH: Science—Miscellanea—Juvenile literature. | Fraud in science—Juvenile literature.
Classification: LCC Q175.37 E455 2018 | DDC 507.2—dc23

Editorial Director: David McNamara
Editor: Michael Sciandra
Associate Art Director: Amy Greenan
Production Coordinator: Karol Szymczuk

PHOTO CREDITS
The photographs in this book are used by permission and through the courtesy of:
Alex Israel, Anton Raath, Associate Press, ASA_Barry Wilmore, CERN, MSU Museum, Damir Grgic, Dreamstime, Edward Larson, Henrique Alvim Correa, Istock, Library of Congress, Louis Bloomfield, Max Resdefault, Museum Paris, NASA, NASA_JPL-Caltech, NASA_Kathryn Hansen, NASA-GPN, NASA-Rogelio Bernal Andreo, NASA, MGS, JPL, NASA/DMSP, Orlando-Ferguson, Rolf Liefeld, Shutterstock, Thinkstock, Urbain-Le-Verrier, Yanornis, Zhaoianus

22MEDIAWORKS (www.22mediaworks.com)
President: Lary Rosenblatt
Designer: Fabia Wargin Design
Editor: Susan Elkin
Writers: Charles Piddock, Susan Taylor, Susan Elkin, Bonnie McCarthy
Copy Editor: Laurie Lieb
Photo Researcher: David Paul

Many thanks to Amy Bauman and Kevin Broccoli for editorial support.

Cover design by Scott Erwert.

Printed in the United States of America

Contents

The Way Stuff (Doesn't) Work

CHAPTER **1**

Neutrinos Are Faster than Light

According to Einstein, nothing can travel faster than the speed of light. But for a brief moment, the world dared to hope otherwise.

A look inside CERN at the Large Hadron Collider. CERN continues to perform experiments with neutrinos.

Photons, or particles of light, travel through a vacuum at the speed of 186,000 miles per second (300,000 kms). But if an object with actual mass were to approach the speed of light, the amount of energy necessary to accelerate it would exponentially increase to infinity—which many have long considered impossible.

In 2011, however, physicists at CERN (Conseil Européen pour la Recherche Nucléaire, or European Center for Nuclear Research) in Switzerland conducted an experiment with neutrinos that seemed to overturn this long-held knowledge. Neutrinos are tiny particles with very little mass that interact so weakly with other particles that they can pass straight through rock. The CERN experiment sent neutrinos from CERN headquarters in Geneva, Switzerland, more than 450 miles (725 km) away to Gran Sasso, Italy. The scientists recorded a speed 60 billionths of a second faster than the speed of light. These findings contradicted Einstein's laws of physics, shocking the world.

Antonio Ereditato, a spokesman for the research team at CERN, announced: "We have high confidence in our results. We have checked and rechecked for anything that could have distorted our measurements, but we found nothing." Nevertheless, the results were too good to be true. Just days after the initial reports, CERN declared the findings false, blaming a faulty cable connection between a GPS and a computer.

So neutrinos aren't faster than light—why did this make people so upset? Because Albert Einstein had famously declared that, if we could somehow find a way to travel faster than light, we could travel through time. So the faulty experiment briefly taunted scientists with the possibility of time travel. It also forced them to reconsider the most basic ideas about our universe.

The error may have been embarrassing to a few scientists, but good work at CERN still continues. In 2012, they discovered a particle that may prove to be the elusive and long-hunted Higgs boson, which scientists believe will explain several mysteries of physics.

Diamonds Come from Coal

Ask a few strangers on the street where diamonds come from, and they'll likely respond: "From coal." Intense pressure, they'll say, turns the coal into shiny, hard, and valuable gems. You then get to revel in busting them, because they're totally wrong.

The misconception may stem from the fact that both coal and diamonds are forms of carbon. While that's true, most diamonds formed long before the plants that later decomposed and formed coal even appeared on Earth.

To find the origin of most natural diamonds, you have to go back billions of years, to when Earth first formed. At the time, carbon was most likely trapped inside the planet's mantle, 100 miles (160 km) below the surface. Over time, intense pressure from the rocks above the mantle, plus temperatures

reaching 2,000 degrees fahrenheit (1,000°C), made some of the trapped carbon crystallize into diamonds. The process for diamond production occurs not everywhere in the mantle, but usually beneath Earth's relatively stable continental plates.

Some time in the past, powerful volcanic eruptions deep underground brought the diamonds to Earth's surface. The stones sat in the magma, which cooled around them and created igneous rocks called kimberlites. While these rocks contain other minerals, it's the diamonds within them that mining companies seek.

Although most of the world's diamonds are found in kimberlites, tiny numbers form in other ways. Some small diamonds have been found in subduction zones, the areas where one of Earth's tectonic plates moves beneath another. Coal could be a source of the carbon involved but other minerals could be, too. The impact of asteroids and meteorites on Earth can also create diamonds. One large deposit in Russia is the result of an asteroid collision some 35 million years ago. The gems, though, are tiny and aren't the quality of diamonds produced deep within Earth billions of years ago.

Rough diamonds on a miner's hand in South Africa.

Alchemy Creates Gold

Myth #3

Before the 19th century, alchemy was a respected pursuit. Using natural elements, alchemists attempted to transmute base metals, such as lead, into noble metals, such as gold. But the mythical substance that would bring about this change—the elixir of life or "philosopher's stone," as it was called—remained elusive. Today, the "science" of alchemy is ridiculed by mainstream and modern scientists.

Alchemists experimented with natural minerals, including sulfur, pyrite, lead, graphite, and more. Although their single-minded obsession with gold didn't pay off, they did make valid scientific contributions to many fields. Their work

improved metalworking, gunpowder, inks and dyes, and medicines. They perfected distillation, the process of purifying a liquid through heating and cooling, and they discovered mineral acids and alkalies, as well as superior distilled spirits. Alchemists inspired Robert Boyle, one of the fathers of modern chemistry, who defined chemical elements (including oxygen, hydrogen, and carbon) based on alchemy's description of the four elements (earth, wind, fire, and water). Even Isaac Newton built on the alchemist theory that all matter contains distinct elements when he discovered that white light contains many colors of the rainbow

when shone through a prism. By today's standards, alchemy is a pointless endeavor, but during the medieval and Renaissance periods, it provided many

serious scientists with nascent ideas that led to later breakthroughs.

Another field to benefit from the early science was chemistry, which evolved from alchemy in both name and practice. Alchemists studied metals and natural minerals in the same way that chemists do today. The scientific method has improved and we now know more about the properties of metals. But alchemy did perform a miracle—transforming magic into practical science.

Heavy Objects Fall Faster

One of the most common misconceptions about physics is that heavy objects fall faster than light ones. At first thought, it seems to make sense: Gravity surely pulls harder on more massive objects, so they should accelerate faster than lighter objects. Drop a feather and a rubber ball, and the rubber ball will reach the ground first. Case closed, right?

Not so fast. As Galileo Galilei, Issac Newton, and other physicists of the Scientific Revolution discovered, the rate of acceleration caused by gravity is independent of an object's mass.

The notion that heavier objects fall faster goes back to Aristotelian physics. The classical philosopher believed that it was the nature of all earthly objects to move toward the center of the universe (which back then was considered the center of our planet). Of the four "common elements" that scientists once believed the world was made of (earth, water, wind, and fire), earth was the heaviest. The more earth an object contained, the heavier it was and the more it would be enticed toward the center of our planet.

Aristotle had his detractors, of course. The Roman philosopher Lucretius wasn't convinced, arguing that weight should have no effect on a falling object's acceleration. The Flemish mathematician Simon Stevin argued the same. It was Galileo, however, who formalized in his *Discourses and Mathematical Demonstrations Relating to Two New Sciences* that all falling objects increase in speed at a rate of the square of the elapsed time. In other words, the velocity of two falling objects—in a vacuum—increases at a known multiple of itself regardless of how heavy the objects are.

Close to Earth's surface, that multiple is a known value of approximately 32.2 feet per second (9.8 meters per second), per second. If you were to drop two objects in a vacuum, no matter how heavy they were, after one second they would be moving at a velocity of approximately 22 miles per hour (32.2kph). After another second they would be moving at the square of that value: about 215 miles per hour (346 kph).

So why did the feather accelerate more slowly than the rubber ball in our experiment? Wind resistance. Galileo's theory requires that the objects fall in a vacuum, but in the everyday world, the air around us exerts a force on falling objects known as drag. Drag slows the acceleration of falling bodies, causing those with a greater surface area to fall more slowly—a notion of comfort to skydivers!

A Pinch of Salt Makes Water Boil Faster

Myth #5

Waiting on the water for your pasta to boil? Cooking magazines and amateur chefs often recommend a simple trick: throw in a dash of salt to shorten the wait. But, even though Grandma swears by that pinch of salt in her famous spaghetti, this trick is not all it's cooked up to be.

In fact, throwing in a bit of salt may have the opposite effect. Salt actually *raises* water's boiling point—the temperature at which a liquid begins to boil—by a tiny amount, meaning that the salted water will come to a boil more slowly than if it were left unsalted.

But even this change is so slight that it might not affect what time dinner hits the table. The boiling point of water is 212°F (100°C). If you add 4 teaspoons (19.72 ml) of salt to 1 gallon (3.7 L) of water, the boiling point will rise to 212.7°F (100.4°C)—which is barely enough to make a difference in meal time.

So how did this myth find its way into the tried-and-true mantras of culinary test kitchens? Once the water's boiling point has been elevated by salt, the water boils at a higher temperature—which can, indeed, cut down a little on cooking time.

Another benefit to this old wives' tale? Adding salt to water after it is already boiling will provide flavor. Pasta absorbs the salty water, leading to a tastier dish.

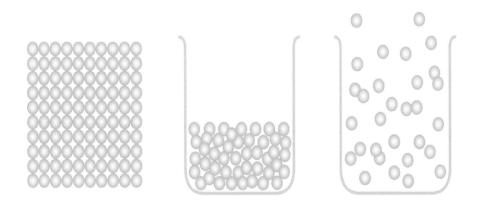

| Solid | Liquid | Gas |

The Three States of Matter

Myth #6

You likely learned in school that there are three states of matter: solid, liquid, and gas. Turns out it's not quite so simple as your textbooks made it seem.

You deal with the three states of matter every day. Ever enjoyed homemade iced tea? You pour liquid water into a teapot, jump when you hear gaseous water screaming out of the spout, and then add solid water—ice—to your tea after you have steeped it sufficiently. But despite what you read in your middle-school science textbooks, there are more than three states of matter.

At the very least, those texts did you a disservice by leaving out plasma. Not to be confused with the biological liquid in which blood cells are suspended, plasmas are a lot like gases in that they exist at a higher temperature than the other states and are amorphous and expand to fill their containers. However, plasmas are very *unlike* gases in that the substance is so hot that electrons that once belonged to individual atoms in a gas now flow freely among themselves.

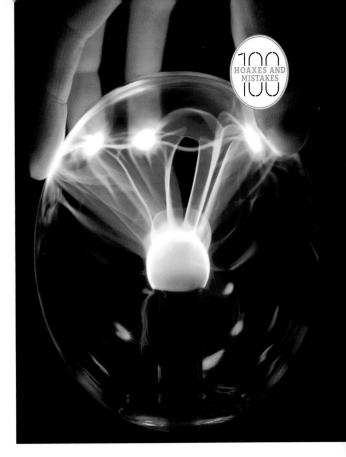

Plasma

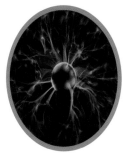

This behavior results in some very odd properties, including luminescence and a keen sensitivity to magnetic fields.

Just as we deal with solids, liquids, and gases, we deal with plasmas every day. Gases excited to the plasma state by electricity are what generate light in fluorescent and neon lamps. When you see an electric spark, either the small-scale sparks that cause shocks in a dry environment or a terrifying, miles-long bolt of lightning, what you're seeing is air transformed into plasma. The light from the sun and every other star in the universe is the result of plasmas created by nuclear fusion. The abundance of plasma in stars means that plasma is the most prevalent state of matter in the visible universe.

While solid, liquid, gas, and plasma constitute the four *classical* states of matter, as is often the case the story changes when we delve into quantum mechanics. Albert Einstein and contemporary Indian physicist Satyendra Nath Bose hypothesized that at a very cold temperature—near absolute zero—matter can reach a state called condensate. Condensates can exhibit weird properties, such as superfluidity (lack of friction) and superconductivity (lack of electrical resistance). While condensates were once merely hypothetical, scientists created the first Bose-Einstein condensates in 1995, meaning there are at least *five* distinct states of matter that scientists have successfully observed. Tell *that* to your sixth-grade science teacher.

Red Mercury Exists

Myth #7

Depending on who you talk to, red mercury was a Soviet-era alternative to the paint that made the B-2 stealth bomber invisible to radar. Or it was a crucial component of the Soviet ballistic missiles' guidance system. Or maybe it's a superconductor in high-precision explosives.

Red mercury is a lot of things to conspiracy theorists and would-be terrorists, but most likely—as a spokesman for the International Atomic Energy Agency (IAEA) put it—it's "a bunch of malarkey." Rumors of the mythical substance have circulated since the late 1980s and picked up steam after the dissolution of the Soviet Union in 1991, when con men posing as rogue nuclear scientists tried selling red mercury to anyone interested in building a nuclear weapon on the cheap.

Every few years, police and international authorities catch dealers trying to buy or sell so-called red mercury—usually a metal or combination of metals that may or may not contain mercury. In early 2015, police in Bangalore posing as buyers caught three men trying to sell a block of aluminum that they claimed was red mercury from Russia. Prices for red mercury are rumored to run absurdly high, in the range of several hundred thousand dollars per kilogram.

If red mercury is real in any sense of the word, it was probably as a code name for lithium-6, a fusible fuel for Soviet thermonuclear weapons. Even if it is just a hoax, however, it may be a useful one. Conspiracy theorists believe that the US government and the IAEA invented the myth of red mercury as a means of sussing out buyers for nuclear material and technology that leaked following the fall of the Soviet Union. Even in the case of would-be nuclear terrorists, the doctrine of caveat emptor ("let the buyer beware") prevails.

Myth #8

Cold Fusion

In 1989, Stanley Pons of the United
States and Martin Fleischmann of
England made a startling claim: they
had successfully produced energy
through a process of cold fusion,
the theoretical idea that a nuclear
reaction can be produced at room
temperature.

Pons and Fleischmann's experiment
used heavy water, meaning its normal
hydrogen atoms had been replaced with
deuterium, a heavier form of the element.
The scientists claimed to have passed a
current through the water from a palladium
cathode and created energy.

The claim drew almost immediate
criticism. Nuclear fusion powers the sun
and other stars and occurs at extremely
high temperatures—100 million degrees
Celsius. As the name suggests, the energy
comes from the fusing together of hydrogen
nuclei. Cold fusion, or low-energy nuclear
reaction (LENR) as the process is now
called, is hypothetically possible, but
other scientists could not replicate Pons
and Fleischmann's experiment. The other
scientists didn't call the original experiment
and its results a hoax; instead, most blamed
Pons and Fleischmann's sloppy methods
and inaccurate record keeping for the
lack of similar results.

In the decades since, engineer Andrea Rossi of
Italy said he successfully created energy using
a LENR system he called the Energy Catalyzer
(E-Cat). Rossi first made his claim in 2011 and
insisted his system was almost ready for
commercial use. Many scientists, though,
distrusted Rossi, as he did not share the science
behind his creation or let them examine it. A

2014 study seemed to verify some of Rossi's
assertions, though, skeptics noted that it was
not an independent test, as Rossi was present at
the time. Some detractors also noted that Rossi
is a convicted criminal, guilty of tax fraud and
dumping environmental toxins, and is known for
past failures in energy production schemes.

Still, another study released in 2015 said
that a version of the E-Cat made from
information taken from media accounts did
produce energy. To many skeptics, however,
the E-Cat is not a credible source of energy,
and cold fusion remains only hypothetical.

Myth #9

N-rays

In 1895, Renee Blondlot— a scientist studying radiation at the University of Nancy in France— announced that he had discovered a new form of radiation he called the N-ray.

I n his lab, Blondlot generated X-rays and aimed them at a quartz prism. Scientists already knew the prism would not reflect the rays, but Blondlot noticed out of the corner of his eye that his radiation detector—a thread covered with calcium sulfide—grew brighter. Something had reflected off the prism and struck the detector. Since it couldn't be an X-ray, Blondlot deduced it was another form of radiation, which he christened the N-ray.

The magazine *Nature* sent American physicist Robert Wood to Blondlot's lab to investigate N-rays and their discoverer. As Blondlot began to demonstrate the existence of the rays in a darkened room, Wood secretly removed the prism from the setup. When Wood asked Blondlot if the rays were still present, the French scientist said yes. But that was impossible, since the prism was supposedly crucial for detecting the rays.

For most scientists, Wood's report marked the end of experimenting with N-rays. It remains a cautionary tale regarding self-deception.

"N" RAYS

A COLLECTION OF PAPERS COMMUNICATED
TO THE ACADEMY OF SCIENCES

WITH ADDITIONAL NOTES AND INSTRUCTIONS FOR
THE CONSTRUCTION OF PHOSPHORESCENT
SCREENS

BY
R. BLONDLOT
CORRESPONDENT OF THE INSTITUTE OF FRANCE
PROFESSOR IN THE UNIVERSITY OF NANCY

TRANSLATED BY
J. GARCIN
INGÉNIEUR E.S.E., LICENCIÉ-ÈS-SCIENCES

WITH PHOSPHORESCENT SCREEN AND OTHER
ILLUSTRATIONS

LONGMANS, GREEN, AND CO.
39 PATERNOSTER ROW, LONDON
NEW YORK AND BOMBAY
1905
All rights reserved

Background images, shown here: Images from Blondlot's 1904 article, "Registration by Photography of the Action Produced by N-Rays on a Small Electric Spark," without N-rays at top and with N-rays at bottom.

The Dangers of Dihydrogen Monoxide

Since the early 1980s, a dedicated group of citizens has waged a crusade against one of the world's deadliest killers: dihydrogen monoxide. Also known as hydrogen hydroxide, hydric acid, or just plain DHMO, this chemical can be lethal if inhaled. But here's the thing: dihydrogen monoxide is water.

Researchers have found DHMO in cancerous tumors as well as acid rain. It contributes to the greenhouse effect, tropical cyclones, and soil erosion. Entrenched interests have prevented the regulation of DHMO, without which industrial solvents, animal research, and nuclear power would be impossible. At this point, you may not find it surprising that Congress is unwilling to take action, leading to rumors that its members themselves may be taking dihydrogen hydroxide.

It all started out as an April Fool's joke in a local newspaper in Durand, Michigan. On April 1, 1983, the *Durand Express* reported that the chemical "dihydrogen oxide" was present in the town's water supply, a substance that produces "vapors [that] cause severe blistering of the skin." Students at the University of California, Santa Cruz, picked up the hoax and ran with it, founding the Coalition to Ban Dihydrogen Monoxide. The "movement" inspired Nathan Zohner, a junior high student in Idaho, to circulate a petition among high school freshmen seeking to ban DHMO. Of the 50 students he solicited, 43 signed, and only one recognized that dihydrogen monoxide is ordinary water.

The ruse continues to circulate in email chains and science classrooms and occasionally nabs a clueless legislator or frightens an uninformed group of people. In 2004, a paralegal nearly convinced city officials in Aliso Viejo, California, to ban polystyrene cups because DHMO was a key component in their production.

In 2007, a New Zealander convinced a member of the parliament to raise the issue on the floor, much to that member's embarrassment. More recently, two Florida DJs landed in hot dihydrogen monoxide for warning listeners about DHMO in their water supply.

While sometimes disruptive, the dihydrogen monoxide prank serves a purpose: it reminds us of our suggestibility in the face of manipulative, scientific-sounding but not particularly scientific misinformation. Thankfully, another fictitious pressure group, Friends of DHMO, reminds us that the substance is natural, environmentally safe, and very refreshing. Just don't listen to anyone who says you need to drink eight glasses of dihydrogen monoxide every day: that one's a myth, too.

Y2K Will End the World

Myth #11

In the months before the new millennium, analysts speculated about an enormous computer network crash that would wreak widespread destruction, giving anti-technology advocates a reason to cluck their tongues and say "I told you so."

Their predictions were based on a lack of foresight by the earliest computer programmers. When computers first went mainstream in the 1970s, many programmers used the last two digits to indicate a year, not allowing for the fact that the first two digits would not always be 19. As the year 2000 approached, many people feared that computers might register the new millennium as the year 1900, causing confusion and massive shutdowns. Speculators envisioned power outages, banking failures, and planes falling from the sky.

President Bill Clinton addressed the problem in a 1998 speech. "No one will ever find every embedded microchip, every line of code that needs to be rewritten. But if companies, agencies, and organizations are ready, if they understand the threat and have backup plans, then we will meet this challenge." For months leading up to January 1, 2000, computer wizards updated their systems to include 20 as the first two digits in the date. Other than a few problems in Japan's nuclear plants and a small disruption for American intelligence satellites, few complications occurred. Thankfully, most people woke up on January 1, 2000, with a hangover as their biggest problem.

Although we sidestepped a global shutdown, another glitch similar to Y2K may rear its head on January 19, 2038, at 3:14:07 UTC (coordinated universal time). Many computers still operate on a 32-bit system,

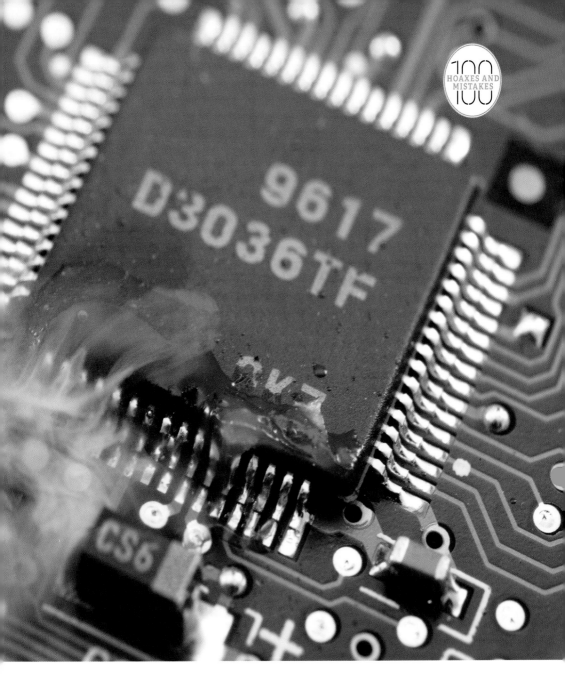

referring to the way a computer processor handles information. These systems use a binary code to track time as a running tally of elapsed seconds, beginning on January 1, 1970, at 12:00:00. But a 32-bit system can only handle a value up to 2,147,483,647, which is exactly how many seconds will have elapsed between January 1, 1970, and January 19, 2038. This bug will cause systems to read the day as December 13, 1901. Luckily, programmers have already started updating computers to a larger 64-bit system, hopefully staving off a massive computer shutdown ... for another 292 billion years, at least.

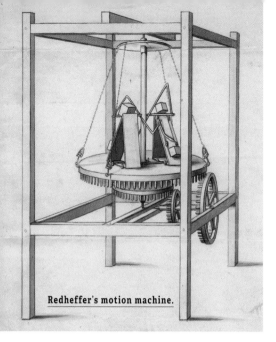

Redheffer's motion machine.

The Perpetual Motion Machine Myth #12

People have long dreamed of a perpetual motion machine—a device that, once set into motion, could keep running forever without requiring additional energy to power it.

Of course, depending on the exact configuration of the machine, it would contradict either the first law of thermodynamics, relating to the conservation of energy, or the second, which addresses entropy. The fact that a perpetual motion machine would contradict these laws of physics does not seem to deter those who insist on its possibility.

It certainly didn't bother inventor Charles Redheffer, who in 1812 came to Philadelphia claiming to have built a perpetual motion machine.

Redheffer charged admission for people to see his seemingly amazing invention, and he asked the state of Pennsylvania to fund another version of it. State inspectors came early in 1813 to examine the machine. However, Redheffer prevented them from entering the room where the machine was kept, claiming that the door was locked and he had misplaced the key.

Inspectors peered through a window to watch the machine work. One of them had brought his son, and the boy noticed something odd. The teeth on the machine's turning wheels were worn opposite the way they should have been if the central

perpetually turning mechanism was powering another gear. In fact, this output shaft, or other gear, was actually powering the central mechanism, not vice versa as Redheffer claimed. The boy's father determined that Redheffer's invention was a hoax, though he couldn't tell how Redheffer had pulled it off.

Seeking greener pastures for securing funds, Redheffer took his machine to New York. There, engineer Robert Fulton, the developer of the steamboat, saw that the gears did not turn evenly. Fulton knocked away some pieces of wood that surrounded the machine, revealing a belt attached to the central mechanism. The belt, Fulton soon realized, was attached to a crank in another part of the building, where an old man was turning the crank by hand. Redheffer was finally exposed as a fraud. But that has not stopped schemers since then from claiming they have perfected a perpetual motion machine.

It's Possible for a Planet to Have Only One Magnetic Pole

Myth #13

All magnetic fields, including the one on Earth, have a north and south pole. But according to electromagnetic theory, there's no reason why a magnet must always have two opposite charges.

South magnetic pole

Compass

Geographic north pole

Magnetic axis

Rotation axis

S N

Crust
Stiffer mantle
Liquid outer core
Solid inner core

Geographic south pole

Magnetic field lines

North magnetic pole

In 1931, theoretical physicist Paul Dirac first described the possibility of a "monopole," defined as an isolated magnet with only one magnetic pole (a north pole without a south or vice versa), and since then physicists have searched for a naturally occurring example. In 1982, researchers at Stanford University in California thought they detected a monopole during an isolated experiment in their laboratory, but no one was able to replicate their findings. More recently, several researchers from Amherst College created synthetic magnetic monopoles using extremely cold atomic gas. But all tests on naturally occurring elements, such as lunar rocks and ancient minerals, turn up negative.

Finding a natural magnetic monopole, if it exists, continues to intrigue scientists. While quantum mechanics say it is possible, all practical applications have failed. For example, if you cut a bar magnet in half, logic suggests that there'd be just one pole in each piece. Instead, each piece has its own north and south pole. Even if you keep chopping that magnet into smaller and smaller pieces all the way down to a single atom, there will still be a north and south pole on that atom. Inside an atom, protons and electrons carry a positive and negative charge.

On a broader scale, Earth behaves the same way. Scientists don't completely understand where Earth's magnetic field originates, but most believe it comes from the rotating liquid core at the center of the planet. This magnetic field protects us against harmful radiation from the sun. It also aids in navigation. Point a compass in any direction, and the tiny magnetic needle will swivel toward the closest pole, pulled by the magnetic attraction between the opposing charges. In the Northern Hemisphere, the compass needle points north; in the Southern Hemisphere, the needle points south. These poles are not stationary; they move around from year to year due to the swirling motions of molten metal in Earth's outer core. Every hundred thousand years or so, Earth's magnetic field flips, and north and south trade places. But one thing is for certain—we're not likely to lose a pole any time soon.

Centrifugal Force

Centrifugal motion is a "fictitious" force, though, that doesn't mean it's not real.

The force you feel pulling you to the left of a car turning right or attempting to eject you from a rapidly rotating amusement park ride derives from two Latin words: *centrum*, meaning "center," and *fugere*, meaning "to flee." Accordingly, centrifugal force is one that pushes or pulls you away from the axis of a rotating body.

However, centrifugal force is *not* one of the four fundamental forces of the standard model, which are gravitation, magnetism, the strong force, and the weak force. These forces hold the universe together, from galaxy clusters to atomic nuclei, and they always describe an interaction between two objects. Since centrifugal force does not represent an interaction between two objects, it technically does not qualify.

Pedants will tell you this means that centrifugal force is not a "real" force but merely the equal and opposite reaction of the *centripetal* force, which is the force that pulls you with the turning car or amusement ride rather than away from it. Others say that centrifugal force is just inertia, in that it's simply the experience of continuing to travel in one direction while your vehicle goes on traveling in the other.

In the end, it's not a matter of right or wrong, real or fake, but a matter of frame of reference. To an observer outside of a rotating system, centrifugal force appears as merely a combination of inertia and centripetal motion. However, observers inside a rotating system will discover that they must account for centrifugal force in describing the motion of objects in their frame of reference. In other words, physics inside a rotating frame of reference will necessarily include a force that pushes objects to the outside of that system.

Because it only occurs inside a rotating system, centrifugal force earns the modifier "inertial" or "fictitious." But here the word fictitious doesn't mean nonexistent; it is simply a word that has specialized meaning in the study of Newtonian physics that locates the force in a certain type of system. Ultimately, centrifugal force is very real, depending on where you were, where you are, and where you happen to be going.

Next time you're whipped around on a whirling carnival ride, note how you feel as if you're being pulled or pushed from the center of the ride—that's centrifugal force in action.

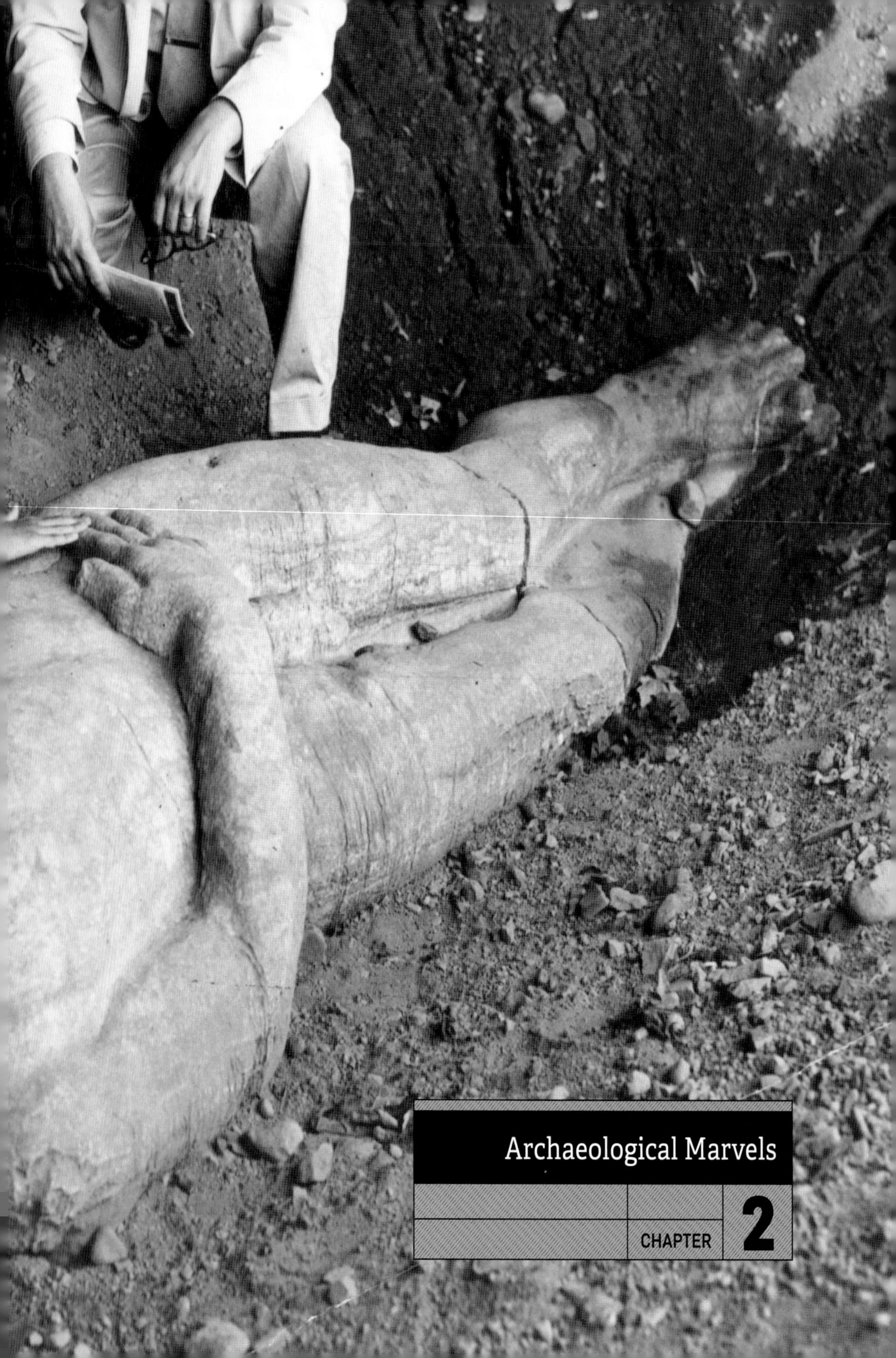

Archaeological Marvels

CHAPTER 2

The Piltdown Man

In 1912, amateur archaeologist Charles Dawson stunned the world. Working with Arthur Smith Woodward, head of geology at London's Natural History Museum, Dawson revealed the existence of what he believed was the so-called missing link in the evolutionary process between apes and humans. The evidence, the two men said, was fossils discovered in Piltdown, England. This alleged human ancestor was soon commonly known as Piltdown Man.

According to Dawson, workers had discovered the fossils over the previous few years. The first were fragments from a thick skull, followed by a jawbone and several teeth. Smith Woodward was convinced the skull fragments had belonged to a human ancestor with a larger skull than an ape, yet the jawbone was more apelike. The blending of the characteristics, Woodward and others believed, confirmed Piltdown Man as the missing link.

At the time, people generally accepted that Piltdown Man was real. But over the next few decades, skeptics emerged. Ancient human fossils were found throughout the world that didn't follow the "missing link" characteristics of Dawson's find. Scientists began to understand that although humans and apes likely shared a common ancestor, their evolutionary paths diverged at some point. Finally, new scientific technology revealed that Piltdown Man was a hoax. In 1949, paleontologist Kenneth Oakley used fluorine dating, a process he had created,

to discover that the skull and jaw fossils were only about 50,000 years old, not 500,000 as Smith Woodward had thought. Other chemical tests revealed that the teeth and the jaw were not the same age as the skull. And with further study, scientists learned the full extent of the hoax: The skull was human and less than 1,000 years old. The jaw and teeth had belonged to an orangutan. The teeth had

It took more than 40 years before Piltdown Man was revealed to be a fraud. A 1913 drawing imagined how Piltdown Man would have appeared.

been filed to make them look more human. And some of the fossils had been stained or painted to make them look older than they were.

Revealing the evidence in 1953, Oakley and several collaborators said Woodward had been the victim of a hoax "so entirely unscrupulous and inexplicable as to find no parallel in the history of paleontological discovery." But neither they nor anyone else since has been able to prove if Dawson duped Smith Woodward or if someone else tried to fool the world with Piltdown Man.

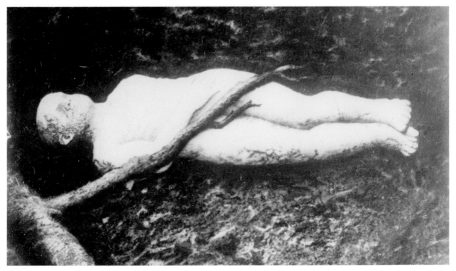

The Cardiff Giant Myth #16

Was it a petrified prehistoric man? Or a work of art carved by an ancient people? For a brief time, 19th-century Americans puzzled over the stone giant unearthed in Cardiff, New York. Ultimately, the "Cardiff Giant" was found to be a hoax, a moneymaking scheme that was moderately successful.

The giant made his first public appearance in October 1869 when Cardiff farmer William Newell hired two men to dig a well. The workers hit stone and uncovered a figure just over 10 feet (3 meters) tall. The area had yielded fossils before, so a theory arose that the Cardiff Giant was the petrified remains of a lost race. Another idea was that the figure was a piece of ancient art. Meanwhile, as experts debated the giant's origins, newspapers heralded the find, and people flocked to Cardiff, paying 50 cents to see it.

As Newell collected admissions fees and famed showman P. T. Barnum inquired about buying it for his museum, some people questioned the giant's true heritage. A mining engineer noted that gypsum, which the giant was made of, would not have endured the wet soil of the Cardiff region. Yale University paleontologist O. C. Marsh examined the giant and declared, "It is of very recent origin and a decided humbug."

The truth behind the Cardiff Giant came out within a year. The hoax was the work of George Hull, who in 1868 had hired two Chicago carvers to create the statue. Hull tried to age it with sulfuric acid and paint. He then enlisted Newell into his scheme. The farmer helped Hull bury the giant and then waited for Hull's word to arrange for its discovery. Hull, an atheist, had seen the hoax as a way to make money and to tweak some Christian fundamentalists who believed, as the Bible said, that a race of giants had once lived on Earth.

Although the hoax was short-lived, the Cardiff Giant remains. The statue is on display at the Farmers' Museum in Cooperstown, New York.

The Lying Stones

A bitter rivalry among university colleagues sparked one of the most embarrassing scientific errors of the 18th century. Johann Beringer was a professor at the University of Würzburg in Germany, where his colleagues described him as arrogant and gullible. He often searched the countryside for fossils and in 1725 came into possession of some surprising remains.

Beringer had employed some local boys to excavate and explore an area of particular interest to him. When the boys brought him stones with images of suns, plants, and birds, Beringer knew they were something special. When more stones were uncovered, this time with Syrian, Hebrew, and Babylonian inscriptions, the professor interpreted his find as a message from God.

Beringer placed so much conviction in his fossils that even while murmurs of a hoax spread throughout the city, he remained committed to publishing theories about the stones' origins. The pranksters, J. Ignatz Roderick and Georg von Eckhart, colleagues at his university, confessed to the entire hoax, but Beringer, convinced that they were jealous of his success, went forward with his

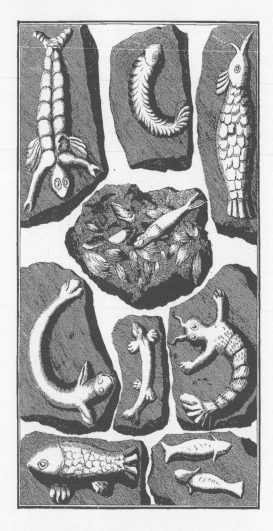

Fake fossils Johann Beringer believed to be "messages from God."

publication of *Lithographiae Wirceburgensis*. Blinded by his belief, Beringer wrote in his thesis, "The figures... are so exactly fitted to the dimensions of the stones, that one would swear that they are the work of a very meticulous sculptor." Finally, after discovering a fossil among the thousands that had been "found" inscribed with his own name, he scrambled to destroy every last copy of his thesis and brought criminal charges against the perpetrators. Beringer won the case and none of the three men ever recovered from the humiliating debacle.

Beringer's discovery is a fitting representation of the 18th-century debate about the origins of fossils. Were they remnants of plants and early animals, pointing to signs of an ancient Earth? Or were they messages from God meant to be decoded according to the Bible? Today, scientists identify fossils using carbon dating, a process in which radioactive emissions of once-living matter are measured to determine its age. Johann Beringer's fossils earned the nickname "lying stones," and the tale serves as a warning to scientists to think outside a single-minded belief and observe all clues before coming to a conclusion.

King Tut's Curse

Myth #18

Did King Tutankhamen, the "boy king" of ancient Egypt, place a curse on his tomb to keep people away from the riches inside? For a time after archaeologist Howard Carter discovered and then unsealed Tut's tomb in 1922, many people thought so, offering several examples to bolster their claim.

The most telling, believers said, was the death of Lord Carnarvon, who paid for Carter's explorations and attended the tomb's opening. The freak combination of a mosquito bite and a shaving nick led to his death: Carnarvon developed a fatal infection. At the time of his death, some British newspapers had already reported on a supposed curse. One quoted Sir Arthur Conan Doyle, creator of Sherlock Holmes and a believer in spirits, as saying the curse was certainly real. Other signs of the curse, some argued, included the seemingly untimely death of others who were at the tomb opening.

Some ancient Egyptians did carve curses into their tombs, hoping to scare away potential grave robbers. Carter himself might have spread the myth of a curse to keep thieves away from Tut's tomb. But there is no scientific proof for the existence of a curse. In 2002, the *British Medical Journal* reported that most non-Egyptians present at the opening did not die unusually early deaths (the curse supposedly didn't affect Egyptians). Carter himself lived 16 years after the opening, and a British guard who stood watch at the site lived for another 60 years.

Scientists have discovered that potentially harmful chemicals and mold exist on some mummies and in unopened Egyptian sarcophagi. But the chemicals' strong smell probably would have deterred Carter if it had been present in Tut's tomb,

and the molds are not dangerous to most people. If anything, human explorers and tourists may pose more risk to the tombs than vice versa. Without proper precautions to safeguard the tombs from exposure, moisture and then mold can fill the tombs and sometimes destroy their contents.

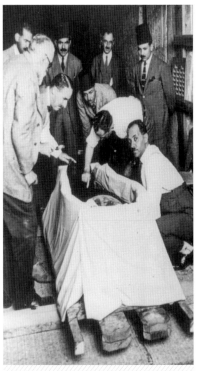

Howard Carter, with magnifying glass, leans over the mummy of King Tutankhamen as the first incision is made in the mummy wrappings.

King Tut's gold and
gem-encrusted
death mask.

The Kensington Runestone

Half a millennium before Christopher Columbus set sail for what he thought would be India, the Viking explorer Leif Erickson became the first European to settle in the New World, establishing the colony of Vinland (in modern-day Newfoundland). Historians and archaeologists believe this to be the farthest west that any European explorer had ventured before the 1500s. But what if that's not true?

The Runestone reads:

"Eight Swedes and twenty-two Norwegians on an exploration journey from Vinland to the west. We had camp by two skerries one day's journey north from this stone. We were out to fish one day. After we came home found ten men red of blood and dead. Ave Maria save us from evil."

In 1898, farmer and Swedish immigrant Olaf Ohlman claimed to have unearthed evidence that Nordic settlers made it far deeper inland than Newfoundland—as far west as his farm in Minnesota. As the story goes, Ohlman found a stone tablet under a tree while clearing his land. Carved into the tablet was a Swedish message, describing an expedition that came to a bloody end in 1362 in what is now the American upper-Midwest. If real, the Kensington Runestone, named for the location of its supposed discovery, is evidence that Nordic explorers ventured farther west than the current historical record indicates.

The Kensington Runestone is certainly a hoax. The tablet's language far more closely resembles the late 19th-century Swedish familiar to Ohlman and his countrymen than the 14th-century Swedish that the mythical explorers would have used. For example, the message uses numerals rather than the spelled-out words for numbers that were common, and it includes terms that Swedish would not borrow from other European languages until the 1700s.

While it's now accepted that the stone is not a real artifact, some individuals in the area still hold onto the idea that Vikings were present in North America before Columbus. Today, the stone is on display in Alexandria, Minnesota.

Shinichi Fujimura and Paleolithic Japan

Shinichi Fujimura is the architect of a Stone Age Japan that probably never existed. The archaeologist once known as "God's Hands" for his success at discovering buried artifacts made headlines in 1981 with the discovery of what was then believed to be the oldest stoneware ever uncovered in Japan.

Over the next two decades, Fujimura uncovered more items that he claimed were far older than any artifacts that other archaeologists had discovered in those regions—or anywhere else in Japan. In 2000, Fujimura claimed to have uncovered the remnants of Stone Age dwellings dating back a whopping 600,000 years, significantly predating any extant artifacts related to human habitation.

But Fujimura was a fraud. The amateur archaeologist so wanted to be the one to discover the oldest relics in Japan that he planted them himself, heading to digs under the cover of night and burying items from his own personal collection. It was the *Mainichi Daily News* that outed Fujimura. Having caught wind of rumors of fraud, the newspaper installed hidden cameras on one of Fujimura's dig sites. Still frames from the video surveillance revealed Fujimura burying artifacts that he intended to "discover" in the light of day.

As Carl Sagan once warned, "extraordinary claims require extraordinary evidence," implying the necessity of greater scrutiny. In this case, scrutiny was lacking for two reasons. First, due to the difficulty of dating stone implements (radioactive dating of stone is unreliable), archaeologists tend to rely on how deep in the earth an artifact was discovered, a measurement that

Fujimura proved easy to fake. The second reason was institutional inertia: nobody in Japan's scholarly community wanted to challenge the man who had generated so much good press for Japan's community of archaeologists. As a result, Fujimura's actions threw into question the entire field of archaeology in Japan, casting doubt on discoveries real and questionable alike.

In fact, artifacts from Paleolithic (Old Stone Age) Japan are distinct. Evidence of human settlement in Japan dates back to at least 35,000 BCE. The Japanese Paleolithic tools are unique in that they are ground and polished, rather than chipped, an innovation that, compared to other Stone Age cultures, was 20,000 to 30,000 years ahead of its time.

Shinichi Fujimura examining "found" artifacts at the sight of one of his digs.

The Tasaday Tribe

In 1972, the cover of *National Geographic* featured a young boy swinging from jungle vines deep in the Philippine rain forest, a member of a presumably undiscovered tribe called the Tasaday.

The 26 members of the tribe had no contact with the outside world, no word for "war," and no idea that other people existed. They dressed in oak leaves and bark, embodying the image of the "noble savage" that many anthropologists identify with the Stone Age. But distrust of the Philippine government as well as oddities in the tribe's behavior caused many scientists to question the authenticity of the Tasaday.

Anthropologists who spent time with the Tasaday noticed inconsistencies between their behavior and the scientists' expectations of a Stone Age society. The Tasaday diet lacked necessary nutrition and their caves were shockingly clean of food waste and human remains. The closest village was only a three-hour bushwhack through the woods, suggesting that even the ancestors of the Tasaday should have had contact with other tribes. A linguistic anthropologist discovered that 80 percent of their vocabulary was similar to the language of nearby Manobo people. The Tasaday had no rituals or folklore, which was strange for a thousand-year-old society. They lived very close to the land, without tools or technology to help them fish or gather food. Controversy surrounded their self-appointed government protector, Manuel Elizalde, an adviser to Ferdinand Marcos, then dictator of the Philippines. The rich and successful Elizalde started a global fund to help the Tasaday but responded to criticism from outsiders by restricting access to the tribe. For nearly a decade, the Tasaday puzzle remained unsolved, though many people were skeptical of their authenticity or curious about their ways. In 1986, when the Marcos regime collapsed, the outside world was able to take a closer look.

In an ABC 20/20 special titled "The Tribe That Never Was," members of the Tasaday confirmed through an interpreter that the tribe is a hoax, its people pawns of politically motivated individuals in a corrupt government. But there were some holdouts, members of the tribe who insisted on their own authenticity. Today, the truth behind the Tasaday is unclear. Anthropologist Thomas Hedland offers one explanation for the naïveté of the tribe but also the apparent flaws in their story. He believes they broke away from the Manobo people sometime in the 19th century, and "perhaps by 1971 the Tasaday really did believe they were the only human beings on the planet." Still others believe that the tribe is merely a small collection of indigenous people living in isolation, perhaps aware of some modern ways but uninterested in altering their way of life.

Anthropologists believe there may be nearly 100 uncontacted tribes around the world with little understanding of our highly industrialized society. Various organizations working to protect these communities focus on making sure logging, mining, and other environmentally damaging industries do not encroach on the ancestral lands of these mysterious peoples.

THE TASADAY TRIBE
WAS BELIEVED TO
BE AN ISOLATED,
UNDEVELOPED SOCIETY
FOR ALMOST 15 YEARS,
BUT ANTHROPOLOGICAL
RESEARCH POINTED TO
A FABRICATION. TO THIS
DAY, THE STORIES AND
THE SCIENCE DON'T
QUITE MATCH UP.

Human Life

CHAPTER 3

Cracking Your Knuckles Gives You Arthritis

Inspired by childhood warnings from his mother that cracking his joints (pulling back on the fingers or pushing down on the knuckles) would cause arthritis, Dr. Donald L. Unger tested the theory by popping the knuckles in one hand, but not the other, for more than 60 years.

After decades of study, Unger published his conclusion in 1998 for the journal *Arthritis and Rheumatism*: "I'm looking at my fingers, and there is not the slightest sign of arthritis in either hand." For his efforts he won the Ig Nobel Prize at a lighthearted ceremony held on the eve of the real Nobel Prizes. Other studies backed him up: cracking your knuckles may annoy other people, but it does not cause arthritis.

Fingers are the most common joint to crack: as many as 50 percent of people share the nervous habit of cracks, pops, and snaps of finger joints. Here's how it works: Articular cartilage covers the ends of two joining bones. Synovial fluid lubricates the joint and cushions the cartilage. As the finger bends, the space between the joints increases, causing dissolved gases in the synovial fluid to form microscopic bubbles. These bubbles merge into larger bubbles that pop as additional fluid rushes to fill the enlarged space between the joints. So why does the relationship between arthritis and knuckle-cracking exist? Some people with arthritis find their joints crack because the cartilage has been damaged. But this seems to be a symptom of arthritis rather than a cause. Typically, arthritis occurs in people with family history, prior accidents, or a lifetime of heavy labor, not a knuckle-cracking habit.

While popping your knuckles may not lead to arthritis, studies suggest that it may cause inflammation and weaken your grip. The damage to your fingers may be minimal, but the annoying habit could put extra strain on your relationships. If that doesn't bother you, crack away.

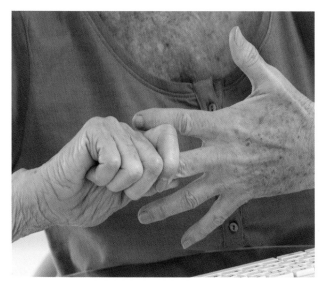

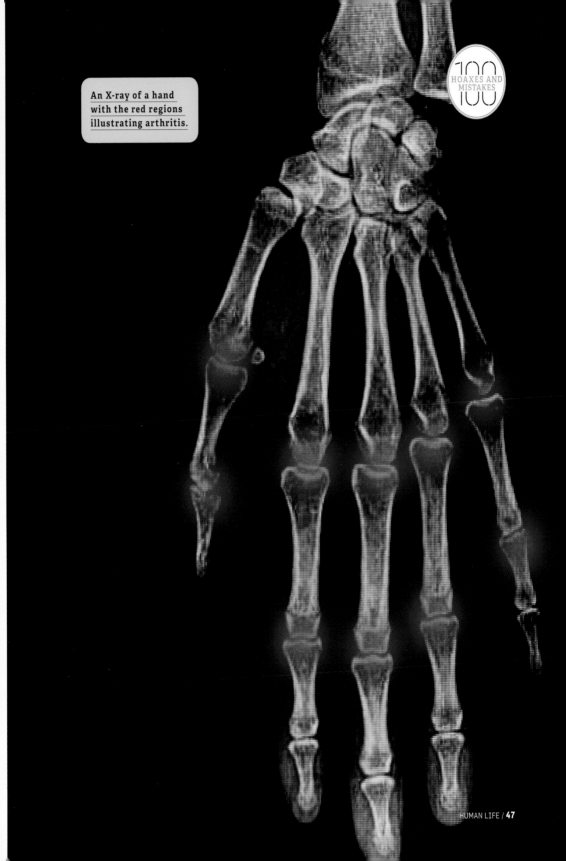

An X-ray of a hand with the red regions illustrating arthritis.

Milk Makes Mucus Thicker

The thick, sticky substance that drips down your throat when you have a cold is called mucus, and it contributes to nasal congestion, hacking coughs, and even snoring. Mucus forms from cells in the nose, sinuses, and lungs. It uses antibodies to trap germs and particles of dirt, so it is working overtime when you have an infection or allergy.

Many people believe that drinking milk will increase mucus production even more so, and to avoid further discomfort you should avoid milk when you're sick.

However, studies from the National Institutes of Health show there is no correlation between milk intake and increased nasal secretions, coughing, nose symptoms, or congestion. Drinking milk may irritate your throat more than water, but it doesn't cause your body to produce more phlegm, says James Steckelberg of the Mayo Clinic. Milk may also thicken saliva, which temporarily coats the throat and gives the impression that there is more mucus. Since other dairy products like cheese don't have the same effect, the texture of milk may be the only culprit for that icky mucus feeling.

In a twist, some doctors even recommend drinking a glass of milk when you're sick, since fluids are then especially important.

A Dropped Penny Can Kill You

Myth #24

Several generations of children have passed along the idea that a penny dropped from a skyscraper could kill someone if it landed on the person's head. Unlike some urban myths, science has a ready tool to disprove this one: it's called terminal velocity. A falling penny will not kill you.

When an object falls, its speed increases, but so does the resistance to its fall from the air around it. That resistance, called drag force, eventually causes the penny to stop accelerating: it reaches its maximum, or terminal, velocity. For a .08-ounce (2.5 g) penny, that speed is about 25 miles per hour (40 kmh), and the penny has to fall only about 50 feet (15.25 m) before hitting that mark.

Physicist Louis Bloomfield of the University of Virginia has studied the dropped-penny problem in a wind tunnel. (For some reason, he couldn't find skyscraper owners willing to let him use their buildings as test sites.) He says that once a penny reaches terminal velocity, it looks more like a fluttering leaf, incapable of harm, than a harmful projectile. "It's very unstable in the air," he says, thanks to the penny's flat shape and very light weight.

What could hurt a little, if not kill someone, would be a penny that fell from a great height in a vacuum. Without the drag force to counteract gravity and the penny's acceleration, the coin could hit a speed topping 200 miles per hour (322 kmh). Luckily, pedestrians don't have to worry about walking in a vacuum and being hit by falling pennies. But they might want to consider the dangers of a ballpoint pen dropped from a tall building. If it fell straight down like a dart, without flipping, it could reach a dangerously high speed of 200 miles per hour (322 kmh) even with drag force, due to its elongated, streamlined shape. Bloomfield says its impact could "chip the sidewalk. It could punch into a wooden board. You wouldn't want it to hit your head."

Cigarettes Are Good for You

Myth #25

In 17th-century Europe, doctors prescribed tobacco as a cure for ailments, including toothaches, fatigue, and joint pains. By the 1900s, many Europeans and Americans smoked cigarettes for enjoyment. But as health scares pervaded the mainstream, tobacco companies fought back, using doctors as a megaphone.

Famous tobacco advertisements in the 1950s even praised the benefits of cigarettes. "More doctors smoke Camels than any other cigarette!" "Toasted to remove throat irritation!" For decades, the smiling faces of doctors and dentists in ads encouraged people to smoke, and since doctors were the authority on health, these statements were hard to ignore. Half of Americans smoked cigarettes in the 1950s. Doctors, encouraged by tobacco companies, continued to endorse cigarette use, even after studies emerged showing the negative correlation between smoking and disease. While the number of tobacco users has significantly decreased, the idea that cigarettes are healthy is one of the deadliest lies doctors ever told.

When rumors spread about the negative effects of cigarettes, tobacco companies took preventive action. They sent sample packs of cigarettes to doctors, many of whom were addicted and expressed doubts about the correlation between tobacco and disease. Patients who showed deteriorating symptoms were prescribed a "healthier cigarette." Some doctors and dentists pictured in the advertisements were paid actors, meant to fool people into thinking cigarettes were beneficial. Tobacco advertising was one of the most dangerous betrayals of the general public of modern times.

It took decades before health authorities set the record straight. Over time, many doctors and organizations stepped up to fight the dangerous lie.

As soon as doctors attributed lung cancer to cigarettes, usage fell from 52 percent in 1954 to 39 percent in 1959, according to *The New England Journal of Medicine*. Finally, in 1964, the US surgeon general announced, "Cigarette smoking contributes substantially to mortality from certain specific diseases and to the overall death rate." New regulations required tobacco companies to put warning labels on all their products. Today, 42 million Americans, or 15 percent of the population, continue to smoke, and the American Cancer Society estimates that 1 in 5 deaths are caused by cigarettes—more than alcohol, car accidents, suicide, AIDS, homicide, and illegal drug-related deaths combined.

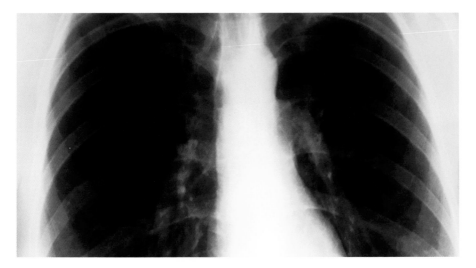

Shaving Makes You Hairier

It's a common myth—some might call it an old wives' tale—that shaving facial or body hair causes that hair to grow back quicker and thicker. The reality is rather different. Hair growth is controlled by the follicle, which resides under the skin. And no amount of shaving is going to affect the follicle.

Think about it: Many people shave their legs with regularity, yet few of them resemble gorillas below the knee. People who are balding are wont to shave their heads, yet said shaving rarely results in a reversal of their follicular fortunes. No scientific study has found that frequently shaving any area of the face—or any other part of the body—has any effect on the thickness, coarseness, or quantity of the hair that grows in that area. (Overwaxing, however, may permanently reduce hair growth by pulling the follicle out of the skin.)

So why does the myth of the bushy beard persist? The reason is due to a flaw in human psychology. Freshly shaven stubble feels coarser simply because longer-lived hairs tend to taper at the ends. We erroneously assume that the act of shaving produced new, thicker hairs, and we ignore future information that refutes this conclusion (a cognitive shortcut known as confirmation bias).

Hope may also play a role. Someone pubescent and itching to grow a real mustache may have few opportunities to speed up the natural biological process, and so they cast about for a reassuring superstition, perhaps provided by a supportive and possibly ill-informed parent. Whether you hang on to this myth out of hope or fear, take it from Dr. Lawrence Gibson, a dermatologist at the Mayo Clinic: "Shaving hair doesn't change its thickness, color, or rate of growth."

Your Fingernails and Hair Keep Growing After You Die

Myth #27

As soon as a person dies, the body starts to shut down, with each organ closing up shop as the oxygen supply to it stops. So how come funeral home workers, transplant surgeons, and grave robbers all tell a grisly tale of hair and fingernails that continue to grow long after the body is dead?

It's true that different cells die at different rates. When the heart does not beat, oxygen supply to the brain stops, and with no glucose, nerve cells die within three to seven minutes. That's why transplant surgeons, who know time is crucial because the body is shutting down, rush to retrieve important organs, such as the kidneys or liver.

Glucose is also a necessary ingredient for fingernail and hair growth. While alive, fingernails grow at a rate of 0.1 mm per day. The germinal matrix, a layer of tissue at the nail's base, produces cells that push the nail upward, contributing to a longer nail. Similarly, glucose drives the hair follicle to produce new cells—about 0.002 inches (0.5 mm) of hair growth a day. But glucose requires oxygen from the beating heart. So when the heart stops, so does the growth of hair or fingernail.

However, coroners aren't lying about a noticeable difference in fingernail or hair length. The skin around the fingernails retracts from dehydration after death, making the nail appear longer. Likewise, facial skin dries out, retracting toward the bone so that chin stubble appears more prominent. Perhaps a postmortem manicure and shave are necessary after all.

Phrenology

The brain remains the organ most impenetrable to human understanding. Since prominent Greek physicians Herodotus and Galen first ascertained that it is the site of the mind, physicians have struggled to understand the relationship between its physical structure and the outward expression of the personality. The pseudoscience of phrenology was the fruit of this struggle.

Austrian doctor Franz Joseph Gall first derived the principles of phrenology in 1798. Gall proposed that the brain is, in fact, a multiorgan structure wherein each of the different organs corresponds to a particular trait of human personality, that the size of each organ determines how powerfully we express that trait, and that a trained physician can measure the size of each organ by feeling the shape of the skull above it. The traits that these brain organs were supposed to control were as varied as constructiveness and destructiveness, love of life, dedication to family, self-esteem, and intellect.

Though Gall was phrenology's father, its chief evangelist was Gall's collaborator, anatomist Johann Spurzheim, whose lectures in Great Britain and the United States were responsible for phrenology's acceptance during the first half of the 19th century. Perhaps the most famous phrenologist, London doctor Bernard Hollander, brought a more quantitative approach to phrenology, determining ways to measure the skull and compare the measurements to the average of the general population.

In fact, it was Hollander's scientific approach to phrenology that set the stage for the misguided discipline's downfall. The subsequent application of the scientific method to phrenology showed that Gall's hypotheses were not borne out by experiment: It became clear that there was no correlation between skull shape and behavior. Gall's brain organs were, in fact imaginary, meaning that the cranial maps phrenologists relied upon were useless. It was telling that phrenologists couldn't even reach agreement on how many brain organs there were (the number ranged between 27 and 40).

Though phrenology eventually gave way to modern psychoanalysis (as pioneered by Sigmund Freud and Carl Jung) and neuroscience, there is a silver lining. Though

not as cut-and-dried as phrenology would have had us believe, and though Gall's map was off, it is now a basic fact of neuroscience that certain physical structures of the brain do in fact control or influence our senses, behavior, and personality.

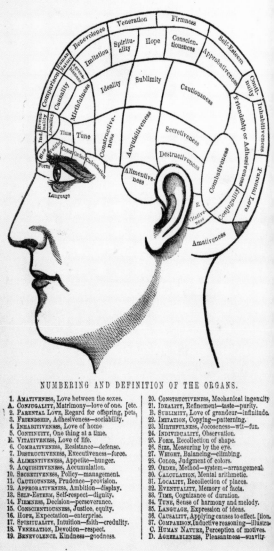

NUMBERING AND DEFINITION OF THE ORGANS.

1. AMATIVENESS, Love between the sexes.
A. CONJUGALITY, Matrimony—love of one. [etc.
2. PARENTAL LOVE, Regard for offspring, pets.
3. FRIENDSHIP, Adhesiveness—sociability.
4. INHABITIVENESS, Love of home
5. CONTINUITY, One thing at a time.
E. VITATIVENESS, Love of life.
6. COMBATIVENESS, Resistance—defense.
7. DESTRUCTIVENESS, Executiveness—force.
8. ALIMENTIVENESS, Appetite—hunger.
9. ACQUISITIVENESS, Accumulation.
10. SECRETIVENESS, Policy—management.
11. CAUTIOUSNESS, Prudence—provision.
12. APPROBATIVENESS, Ambition—display.
13. SELF-ESTEEM, Self-respect—dignity.
14. FIRMNESS, Decision—perseverance.
15. CONSCIENTIOUSNESS, Justice, equity.
16. HOPE, Expectation—enterprise.
17. SPIRITUALITY, Intuition—faith—credulity.
18. VENERATION, Devotion—respect.
19. BENEVOLENCE, Kindness—goodness.
20. CONSTRUCTIVENESS, Mechanical ingenuity
21. IDEALITY, Refinement—taste—purity.
22. SUBLIMITY, Love of grandeur—infinitude.
23. IMITATION, Copying—patterning.
24. MIRTHFULNESS, Jocoseness—wit—fun.
25. INDIVIDUALITY, Observation.
26. FORM, Recollection of shape.
27. SIZE, Measuring by the eye.
28. WEIGHT, Balancing—climbing.
29. COLOR, Judgment of colors.
30. ORDER, Method—system—arrangement.
31. CALCULATION, Mental arithmetic.
32. LOCALITY, Recollection of places.
33. EVENTUALITY, Memory of facts.
34. TIME, Cognizance of duration.
35. TUNE, Sense of harmony and melody.
36. LANGUAGE, Expression of ideas.
37. CAUSALITY, Applying causes to effect. [idon.
C. COMPARISON, Inductive reasoning—illustra-
C. HUMAN NATURE, Perception of motives.
D. AGREEABLENESS, Pleasantness—suavity.

Vaccines Cause Autism

Myth #29

In 2015, an outbreak of measles in California highlighted a small but growing problem: More parents were choosing not to vaccinate their children against common diseases. Some parents believed that the vaccinations increased the risk of their children developing autism.

The alleged link between vaccinations and autism gained a foothold in 1998 after British doctor Andrew Wakefield published the results of a study he had done. Wakefield claimed that the combined vaccine for measles, mumps, and rubella (MMR) increased the chance that a child would develop autism. Scientific critics attacked both his small sample size—just twelve children—and his methodology. The scientific journal that published Wakefield's report later retracted it, claiming it was fraudulent. Dr. Wakefield's license to practice medicine in the United Kingdom was even rescinded.

But the debunking of his report did not stop some parents from using it as a way to explain their children's autism, especially if the children first showed signs of the disorder after being vaccinated. (Coincidentally, many of the outward signs of autism begin to present around the age of vaccination, between 12 and 15 months.) Some anti-vaccine proponents pointed to the potential dangers of a common vaccine preservative, thimerosal, which contains mercury. Concurrent with Wakefield's study, U.S. drug makers began reducing or eliminating the amount of thimerosal in most vaccines for children. That effort, the Centers for Disease Control (CDC) explained, was to reduce children's exposure to all forms of mercury. Today only a handful of flu vaccines still contain the preservative.

The CDC and other health agencies have taken great pains to explain that no studies have linked vaccines to autism. One study in Scandinavia showed that autism rates did not drop after thimerosal was removed from vaccines there, although a drop would have been expected if the preservative was the culprit. Other studies show no difference in the incidence of autism between groups of children given vaccines with thimerosal and those given vaccines without it.

Despite these assurances, some parents still believe in the vaccination-autism link or have other reasons for not vaccinating their children. That decision has increased the spread of measles, once considered eradicated in the United States.

and facts is also personal, depending on our genes, brain development, and attention level when presented with news. But whatever factors shaped our memory, it can never create mental photographs. You'll just have to leave the snapshots to your camera.

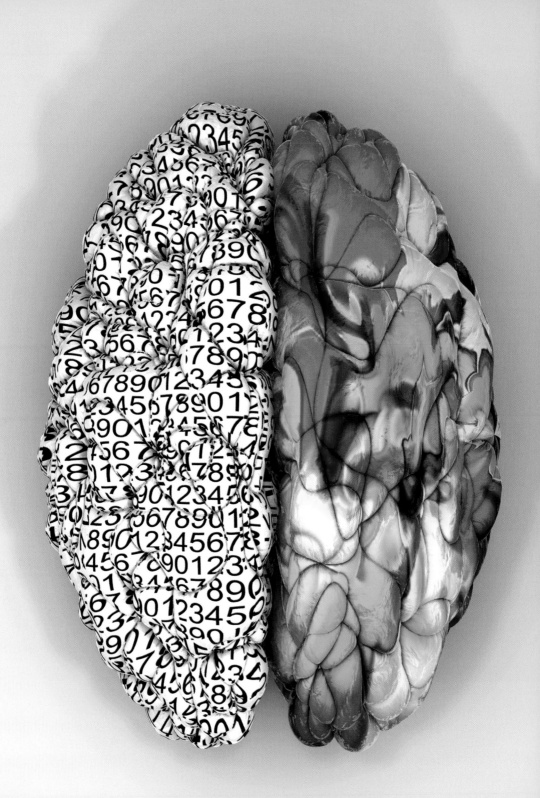

Left Brain, Right Brain— Right? Wrong!

Myth #33

In the 1960s, neuropsychologist Robert Sperry embarked on a research program that eventually won him the Nobel Prize. Sperry's work with split-brain patients—epileptics whose doctors removed the connections between the right and left brain hemispheres to treat their seizures—concluded that a specific half of the brain was more involved in reading, writing, and arithmetic than the other. These findings filtered out into the popular press, and pop psychologists ran with it.

Somehow, Sperry's findings on the "lateralization" of the brain morphed into a belief that creative imagination is controlled by the "right brain" while logical analysis is controlled by the "left brain" and that people are generally right or left brained. This belief has since informed everything from self-help books to occupational aptitude tests. The simplicity of the theory combined with its scientific undertones explains why it has stuck around so long—despite the fact that it's wrong.

Not that there isn't significant evidence for lateralization of the brain. However, this lateralization tends to be more nuanced. While the right hemisphere visualizes shapes and the left hemisphere visualizes details, both are required for interpreting visual information. While the right side is predominant in processing linguistic meaning and the left side is largely responsible for processing grammar, both are necessary for interpreting language. Recent studies of middle school students as they analyzed mathematical problems indicate that the most successful ones were those whose left and right hemispheres communicated the most—not students that showed any particular dominance in one or the other.

The verdict is that while brain lateralization and localization of mental processing are a real thing, these findings do not—and never did—support the idea that creativity and analysis are two ends of a spectrum representing the lateral orientation of the brain. Besides, even those who buy into left- and right-brain theory now believe that success is a combination of both analytical strength and creativity. In other words, you benefit most by using more than half of your brain.

It Takes Seven Years to Digest a Piece of Gum

Gulp. The piece of gum you've been chewing has accidentally slid down your throat, destined to be trapped in your stomach for seven years, immune to the acids that break up your food (or so you've been told since childhood). Research proves that while swallowing gum is not a seven-year sentence, it's not exactly healthy for you, either.

The Food and Drug Administration categorizes gum as a "nonnutritive masticatory substance" composed of synthetic elastomers and rubberlike materials such as butyl rubber, the same ingredient used to make inner tubes. Typically, gum is a combination of gum base, sweetener, flavoring, preservatives, and softeners. In the past, gum makers used chicle, a part of the sapodilla tree, but demand outpaced production, and today most gum is made of natural or synthetic polymers.

Your body is unable to process these materials, but they don't get stuck in your stomach for seven years. Rodger Liddle, a gastroenterologist at the Duke University School of Medicine, told *Scientific American* that "nothing would reside that long, unless it was so large it couldn't get out of the stomach or was trapped in the intestine." (Objects as large as a quarter may pass.) The stomach breaks through some components of gum, such as sugars and mint flavoring, but the gum emerges on the other side mostly intact.

Still, just because you can't find a trash can doesn't mean you should regularly swallow that minty fresh stick. If ingested daily, gum may cause constipation. It could also become lodged in the throat or stuck to other food, preventing it from passing. But the fabled seven-year sentence is false. Gum should pass through your system in as little as a week.

You Lose Most of Your Body Heat Through Your Head

100 HOAXES AND MISTAKES

No winter wardrobe is complete without a hat, and many people believe it's the most important layer. But if your head represents only about 10 percent of your body's total surface area, is it really the most critical body part to keep warm?

Most experts recommend preserving your body heat as long as possible when it's cold outside. "It's easier to keep the heat in than get the cold out," says Quinn Brett, a wilderness guide and emergency medical technician (EMT). That means bundling up wherever skin meets the elements. But your head does not lose any more heat than other parts of your body.

The myth originated in a 1970 US army survival manual that stressed the importance of a hat because you lose "40 to 50 percent of body heat" from the head. The army reached this conclusion through a vaguely scientific experiment in which participants wore Arctic survival suits covering everything but their heads. Not surprisingly, the volunteers' heads felt cold but their bodies did not.

In 2006, scientists revisited the army's experiment and found that heat loss is proportional to the surface area of exposed skin. They dressed participants in wetsuits with varying degrees of coverage. Those without head protection lost between 7 and 10 percent of their body heat—about the same proportion as the surface area of the head compared to the body's total surface area.

That doesn't mean you should trash your supply of warm hats. Shivering is a natural reaction to feeling cold and helps keep you warm. But when just your head is cold, you're unlikely to shiver, meaning it's harder for you to stay warm. You may also feel the cold more severely because the face, head, and chest are more sensitive to temperature changes than other parts of the body. So wear a hat. But a wool hat alone won't save you from the cold, so bundle the rest of yourself up, too.

Cold Weather Can Make You Sick

Myth #36

You may think it's called the common cold for a reason—it happens more frequently during cold months, with the dreaded flu season reaching its peak during the worst months of winter, so many people believe that cold weather contributes to increases in illness. But is there a connection between being cold and having a cold?

According to scientists, germs make you sick, not the cold weather. You need to come into contact with the influenza virus to fall ill. But why does this sickness peak in the wintertime? Human behavior may be to blame. We tend to retreat into warm homes, where central heating can cause nasal passages to dry out and create ideal settling spots for viruses. In close quarters, infected people come into contact with healthy ones, spreading the germs faster than in outdoor environments.

Another factor for your runny nose may be the dry climate. Dry winter air allows the flu and cold viruses to survive and spread. A 2010 study by the National Institutes of Health compared death rates from influenza to humidity ratings around America. Researchers discovered that flu outbreaks spiked after a drop in humidity during the previous weeks.

Understanding how climate contributes to the influenza virus and rhinovirus can help us predict when outbreaks will occur. Hospitals can also discourage the spread of the virus by controlling humidity levels.

However, if you think the cold is actually making you sick, it might not be all in your head after all. A 2015 study at Yale involving rats infected with the rhinovirus showed a slight correlation between a cooler environment and the spread of disease. When temperatures dropped, the immune system performed poorly in general. Scientists have yet to demonstrate this phenomenon in human beings.

Leprosy Is Highly Contagious

Myth #37

The curse of the disease known as leprosy long inspired panic throughout the world. Like many leaders, in an attempt to limit spread of the disease, King Kamehameha V banished Hawaiians diagnosed with the terrible sickness to leper colonies. Between 1865 and 1969, approximately 8,000 people were exiled to the island of Molokai to die.

These patients lived in isolation with disfigured hands and faces, often blind; many died of the disease. Leprosy gained a reputation as highly contagious, devastating, and irreversible. That stigma continues, even though we now know that it is much more difficult to transmit than first believed.

Also known as Hansen's disease, leprosy is an infection caused by the bacterium *Mycobacterium leprae*, which was discovered by Norwegian scientist G. A. Hansen in 1873. The bacterium causes nerve damage, affecting the skin, upper respiratory tract, eyes, and nose, as well as leading to festering wounds and deformities. The bacterium grows slowly inside its host but cannot survive outside, making it difficult to study. Patients often ignore the disease's first signs—pale, painless, and itchless patches on the skin—and it moves so slowly that it can take 20 years for symptoms to appear. Leprosy most likely spreads through sneezing and coughing or through broken skin, but researchers have not yet pinpointed the source. Ability to fight the infection is genetic, so some people are able to stave it off while others are susceptible.

During medieval times, leprosy was very common and the stigma around the disease was a curse worse than death. Those infected had to wear special clothing, ring bells to warn others that they were nearby, and walk on certain parts of the road. The disease all but died out in Europe more than 200 years ago, except for several cases in Norway lasting until the 20th century, though, there are still leper colonies in India, China, and Africa. Today, long-term progression of the disease is rare and doctors can easily treat it with fast-acting antibiotics before disability sets in.

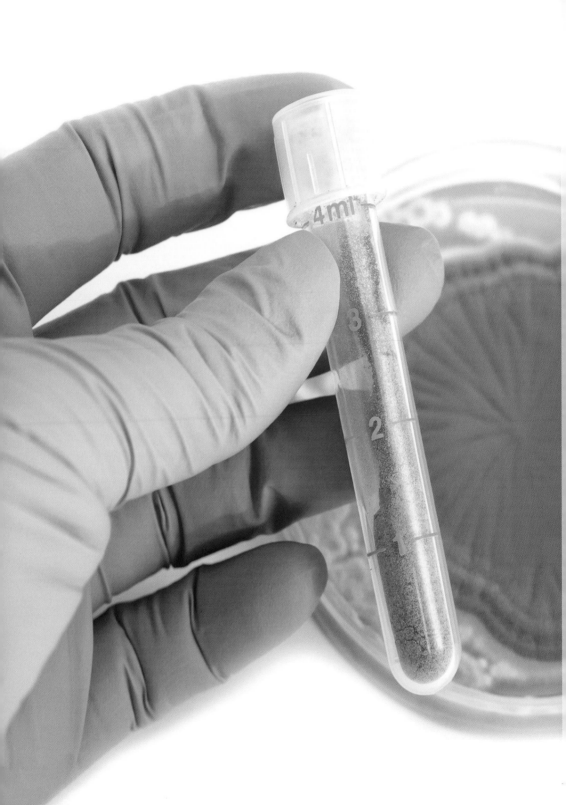

Antibiotics Can Be Used Against Viruses

Antibiotics may be the most important discovery of the 20th century. Thanks to biologist Alexander Fleming's discovery of penicillin and the work of his successors to develop these wonder drugs, diseases like tuberculosis and syphilis, which for centuries had led to gruesome deaths, were suddenly treatable. Unfortunately, this medical miracle applies only to bacterial infections, not viral diseases.

Antibiotics such as penicillin work by weakening the cell walls of bacteria that cause infection or by hindering the bacteria's ability to reproduce. Bacteria are responsible for only a fraction of known infections, while viruses—along with fungi and prions, infectious protein bundles that carry illnesses such as mad cow disease—are responsible for the rest. Viruses, which are not cellular life forms and do not reproduce on their own, are not susceptible to antibiotic treatment.

Sadly, this fact has not stopped doctors from prescribing antibiotics for viral infections. The typical sore throat is a result of a viral infection, but it could also be a harbinger of strep throat, which is caused by streptococcus bacteria. A doctor who prescribes amoxicillin for a sore throat before getting positive results from a strep test is erring on the side of caution—the patient might not come back to the doctor's office before a potential streptococcus infection becomes both dangerous to the patient and contagious to the general population. Or the doctor, after examining a sick child, might just write a prescription to appease the patient—or the patient's parents, who are demanding some treatment.

Whatever the reason, prescribing antibiotics for viral infections is not the innocuous decision it once might have been. The overprescription of antibiotics is, in part, responsible for generating a raft of antibiotic-resistant diseases. When patients take unnecessary antibiotics— or when they stop taking the medication before finishing the prescribed amount—they create an environment in which only the strongest bacteria can survive. This allows bacterial colonies to adapt to and resist the drug they were exposed to. As a result, gonorrhea and tuberculosis are much harder to control today than they used to be, while methicillin-resistant *Staphylococcus aureus* (MRSA) is the scourge of modern hospitals.

It's a natural desire to take medicine—any medicine—when you're sick, especially if there seems to be no other treatment but aspirin and bed rest. But think twice before you demand antibiotics from your physician: you may be breeding the next generation of superbug.

Dubiously trained "surgeons" would perform painful blood-letting procedures, often killing their patients in the process.

Bloodletting Will Make You Well

Blood is vital to our survival, but ancient physicians often used a technique called bloodletting—the process of draining blood from a patient—to cleanse the body of impurities and fluids and cure illness. Today we know that bloodletting killed far more people than it cured, yet it took until the 19th century for the practice to die out.

Bloodletting began as early as 3,000 years ago in Egypt. Physicians drained blood in response to a variety of ailments—from the plague to a bad case of acne. Many people viewed disease as a curse by an evil spirit, and bloodletting allowed the spirit to escape from the body. Physicians often doubled as priests since they assumed unnatural spirits were the cause of disease. But the practice often backfired. Excessive bleeding led to anemia and frequently exposed the patient to more infection.

You may find it surprising, then, to hear that removing blood (now called phlebotomy) is making somewhat of a comeback among modern physicians. Phlebotomy thins the patient's blood and prevents clots and strokes. Physicians sometimes use phlebotomy to treat patients who have too much iron in the blood or overproduce red blood cells. Doctors also use this treatment for metabolic syndrome, frequently diagnosed in people suffering from obesity.

A few modern doctors even use leeches to reattach body parts like fingers and toes. These doctors do not use leeches like their ancient counterparts—to drain the blood of impurities—but instead employ them to help restore circulation, heal skin grafts, and reattach damaged veins.

The small amount of success attributed to bloodletting in the past may have been due to the placebo effect. If patients believed in the therapy, the attitude change may have been enough to buoy them through their illness. Thankfully, science stepped in to save the vast majority.

You Can't Grow New Brain Cells

In 1957, a 74-kiloton atomic bomb detonated during a test at Yucca Flat, Nevada. The blast irradiated carbon in the upper atmosphere, where it became radioactive carbon-14. Carbon-14 reacted with oxygen to form radioactive carbon monoxide, which oxidized further into carbon dioxide, which rode the jet stream for thousands of miles. Finally, a lingonberry shrub in Sweden photosynthesized that carbon dioxide into fructose.

At first thought, nuclear weapons testing seems unrelated to neuroscience, but later, when a sleepy-eyed Swede enjoyed a spot of lingonberry jam with his breakfast, he ingested with it radioactive carbon-14, which his body converted into neurons. The presence of carbon-14 in his brain, discovered by scientists decades later, became the strongest evidence yet that human brain cells continue to replicate well into adulthood.

For decades, neuroscientists believed that we grew all our brain cells in the womb and during early childhood, and that was that. But contradictory evidence appeared in the 1960s and 1980s showing ongoing turnover of brain cells in mice. In the next two decades, neuroscientists found evidence of adult neural cell production in the human hippocampus—the part of the brain responsible for acquiring and storing memories. Despite these new findings, skepticism remained, particularly about how active neural stem cells were in adulthood and whether those new cells contributed at all to neural processing.

It was a study led by Kirsty L. Spalding at the Karolinska Institutet of Stockholm that showed constant regeneration of neurons in the hippocampus through adulthood. Thanks to the spike in Cold War nuclear testing during the 1950s and the resultant increase in atmospheric carbon-14, the team could discern how much of the radioactive isotope people were ingesting during the era and how much of if their bodies deposited in their cells. Since the human body deposits new elements in its cells only when those cells are regenerating, the increased presence of carbon-14 in hippocampal neurons means that those adults must have been generating new brain cells.

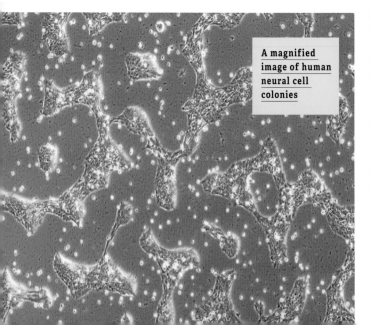

A magnified image of human neural cell colonies

The idea that neurons can form in adulthood brings hope to those suffering from devastating diseases of the central nervous system, such as Alzheimer's, Parkinson's, and Lou Gehrig's disease (ALS). If doctors can learn to harness the body's ability to regrow brain cells, then these horrible afflictions may become more susceptible to treatment. With any luck, science might even find a cure.

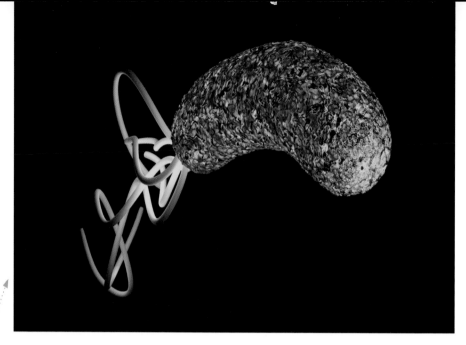

Stress Can Cause Ulcers

Myth #41

It was a common imagine in film and TV several generations ago: The stressed-out executive dealing with stomach pain and heartburn due to ulcers. Common wisdom held that emotional stress triggered symptoms that left patients doubled over in pain and reaching for milk to soothe it. Doctors now know that old-fashioned "wisdom" was wrong. Milk is exactly the wrong thing to give an ulcer sufferer, and emotional stress has no role in the onset of ulcers.

An ulcer is any open sore on the skin or a mucous membrane. In the digestive system, ulcers develop in the esophagus, stomach, or duodenum—the upper part of the small intestine. They are sometimes collectively called peptic ulcers.

In the past, doctors thought emotional stress, along with caffeine and spicy foods, caused ulcers. Then, in 1982, Australian doctors Barry Marshall and Robin Warren identified the spiral-shaped bacteria *Helicobacter pylori* as the cause of most incidences of peptic ulcers. That discovery led doctors to prescribe antibiotics to treat most ulcers and won Marshall and Warren the 2005 Nobel Prize for Physiology or Medicine.

But if *H. pylori* wasn't found to be the sole cause, what else can spur a peptic ulcer? Lifestyle does play a part, as smoking cigarettes can cause ulcers. Other factors, such as taking non-steroidal anti-inflammatory drugs (NSAIDS), like aspirin and ibuprofen, can make the stomach more susceptible to the effect of certain stomach acids that play a part in forming ulcers. (Milk stimulates the production of those acids, which is why it's the wrong tonic for people with ulcers.) As for stress: Some people who already have ulcers say fretting over daily life makes their pain worse. And physical stress, such as going through a major operation, may lead to some ulcers.

Mary Toft's Incredible Progeny

Myth #42

Mary Toft began 1726 as a typical peasant woman in Surrey, England. Within months, she would become an absolute sensation across the country, and by the end of the year, Toft would be one of the most infamous Britons of her time. The source of all the commotion? Rabbits.

Toft, a mother who had recently miscarried, seemed to go into labor just a month after her failed pregnancy in 1726. What she birthed was astonishing: a jumble of animal parts, seemingly from a cat, a rabbit, and an eel. She repeated the feat again a few days later in the presence of the local midwife, John Howard. The grotesque miracle drew attention at the court of King George I. Hoping to witness it with his own eyes, a Swiss surgeon at court by name of Nathaniel St. André headed to the countryside to see Toft once again give birth to several disembodied rabbit parts. He was quickly convinced.

St. André's credulity aside, many physicians were skeptical. Among those skeptics was another of King George's surgeons, Cyriacus Ahlers. Ahlers managed to obtain samples of the rabbits Toft birthed and found knife wounds on their bodies, indicating that the animals had not died inside the woman's womb. Desperate for clarification, the king ordered St. André to bring Toft to London. When she arrived, Toft's unusual labors ceased. She was found out when her sister tried to bribe a porter to sneak a rabbit into her living quarters.

But how was Toft able to get away with such a farce for as long as she did? The theatrics played off a belief called "imprinting," in which experiences during pregnancy can affect one's offspring. Toft claimed that she had chased after and dreamed of rabbits during the time of her miscarriage. It's also likely that St. André was favored by King George for his fluency in German (the king's native tongue) rather than his medical acumen.

When asked why she went through the trouble of producing such an elaborate hoax, Toft said she hoped that the fame would help her rise above her impoverished peasant life. Sadly, she was unsuccessful in this endeavor: Mary Toft died as poor as she lived. As for the doctors who believed her, Howard and St. André ended their careers in predictable disgrace.

MARY TOFTS,
(The Pretended Rabbit Breeder.)

Sugar Causes Hyperactivity

The simplest, most entrenched myths are the hardest to bust, regardless of how false they may be. One of the stickiest myths is that sugar is a major contributor to hyperactivity in children. Parents of young children adhere persistently to this myth, especially around the most sugary day of the year: Halloween. However, study after double-blind study shows absolutely no relationship between sugar consumption and hyperactivity.

It's not clear when, where, or how this myth originated; there's no medical study that seems to have sparked the belief that sugar causes hyperactivity. Though concerns about food additives, sucrose among them, began to take hold in the 1970s, none of the popular press articles covering these matters specifically linked added sugar to rambunctiousness. Nevertheless, it's not difficult to take a logical leap of faith between sugar, a store of energy, and overly energetic children. This is especially true since children tend to eat sugary foods at children's parties and other youthful get-togethers at which they may act particularly boisterous. Heck, even adults are prone to seek out a sugar boost when the early afternoon doldrums hit.

Conventional wisdom notwithstanding, the medical literature is uncommonly clear. A 1995 paper in the *Journal of the American Medical Association* analyzed 23 previous studies, seeking a link between sugar and hyperactivity—no correlation was found. Even more telling, a 1994 double-blind study showed that parents perceived their children to be hyperactive if researchers told them their children had ingested sugar, even if they had consumed no more sugar than the control group.

In other words, the myth of sugar-based hyperactivity perpetuates itself due to self-fulfilling expectations. We expect children to act rowdy when we think they've had sugar, so we interpret and magnify their behavior to fit our expectations. Although this myth is a fairly harmless one, we know today about the real dangers of consuming too much added sugar: cavities, diabetes, and obesity, for starters. The fact that hyperactivity isn't one of those dangers doesn't mean we shouldn't be cutting back.

THE ENERGY BURST THAT YOU SEE HERE WAS NOT—WE REPEAT!—*NOT* BROUGHT TO YOU BY A CANDY BINGE. SCIENTISTS HAVE BEEN DEBUNKING THAT MYTH FOR MORE THAN 20 YEARS.

Humans Evolved From Apes

Humans' evolutionary progress was once thought to be clear: stooped, hairy ape turns into upright Neanderthal wielding an ax, who eventually evolves into hairless human wearing a suit and holding an iPhone.

Even Charles Darwin suspected a common connection between humans and orangutans, a type of ape: "Man in his arrogance thinks himself a great work, worthy the interposition of a deity. More humble and I believe true to consider him created from animals." While it's true we share a common animal ancestor, scientists now believe humans and apes took very different paths.

But, to better understand this myth, let's start with our similarities. We share 98.8 percent of our DNA with chimpanzees, as well as attributes such as compassion for others, aggression, awareness of self, and ability to reason. And both humans and chimps use tools and pass down knowledge to succeeding generations.

However, the similarities pretty much end there. A chimp's brain and skull size, while similar to that of our more recent extinct relatives, is still a quarter of the size of today's human head. Our larger brain size gave us a distinct evolutionary advantage, allowing for more complex language skills and complicated cultural systems. Meanwhile, chimpanzees evolved

to survive in the African Congo, something current humans would struggle to do. Today chimpanzees border on extinction while humans worry about overpopulation.

Fossils of humans' ancestors in Africa reveal a complex lineage, albeit with many gaping holes. Paleoanthropologists have discovered footprints and fragments of femurs and skulls that are sometimes apelike and other times manlike, indicating

Despite strong similarities in our DNA, paleoanthropologists have discovered early human fossils indicating that chimps and humans evolved from a distant relative, hominids, rather than the widely accepted paradigm that humans evolved directly from chimps— rendering this popular image invalid.

that apes and early humans cohabitated in south and east Africa. The puzzle is incomplete, but scientists agree that our direct evolutionary line does not lead back to chimpanzees. Instead, humans and chimps share a common ancestor tracing back five million to eight million years ago. One lineage developed directly into apes like chimpanzees and gorillas, as the other evolved into early human ancestors called hominids. Our direct human ancestors, *Homo habilis* and *Homo erectus*, first hit the scene two million years ago. From that point, humans spread throughout the world, migrating to Europe and later Australia and the Americas. We don't know the number of hominid species that existed, or our relationship with them, but the fossils speak loudly: the chimp at the zoo is not your great-great-great grandad.

Blondes and Redheads Are Disappearing

Myth #45

In 2002, news outlets around the world announced that blondes and redheads would soon be extinct because not enough people carry the recessive genes that cause those hair colors. The sensationalist rumor spread quickly into famous folklore. But many journalists failed to verify the "scientific" source.

Only 2 percent of the world's population can claim blonde as their natural hair color, while only 1–2 percent of the population have the even rarer red hue. The gene that is responsible for determining the pigment of your hair, skin, and eyes is MC1R (melanocortin 1 receptor). Each parent passes along a copy of the MC1R gene, and when one is dominant, such as brunette hair, and one is recessive, such as red or blonde hair, the recessive gene stays hidden. Red and blonde hair are more prevalent in northern European countries, like Scotland and Finland, than elsewhere in Europe, probably because

ancestors from these nations were isolated from other groups. The chance that two recessive gene carriers would meet and reproduce was therefore more common.

It's certainly not unheard of for a recessive gene to die out. Nearsightedness, for example, would die out without modern technology to give the host a boost in the form of glasses. If we lived only by the rules of natural selection, those with poor vision would not be able to hunt, gather, or contribute to society and would likely not procreate, thereby not passing on the gene. Over time as the gene pool adjusts to these changes, the trait would

disappear. So to eliminate blondes and redheads completely, the trait would need to cause an unfortunate disability. Of course, it doesn't, unless you live in Florida and find the sun too powerful for the fair skin that usually accompanies these hair colors. But even that wouldn't keep you from finding a mate, provided you knew the benefits of sunscreen.

The only way for the red and blonde genes to vanish completely is if all redheads and blondes suddenly stopped procreating. All carriers of those genes would need to abstain as well. That probably won't happen any time soon.

It's Dangerous to Wake a Sleepwalker

Myth #46

The classic image of sleepwalkers in films and cartoons shows people slowly lurching forward with their eyes closed and arms outstretched. In reality, sleepwalkers might open their eyes while taking a nocturnal stroll, which can range from sitting up in bed to heading to the kitchen to prepare a meal.

Whatever you've heard about sleepwalking, it probably includes this warning: never wake a sleepwalker. According to lore, disrupting people in an active-somnambulant state can harm or even kill them. Science, though, has a clear response to that claim—hogwash. Sleep specialist Mark R. Pressman puts it succinctly: "It's not dangerous for the sleepwalker to wake him up."

Most sleepwalking takes place early in the night, when the slumberer's brain has yet to enter a deep state of rapid-eye movement

(REM) sleep. Studies show that certain areas of the sleepwalker's brain are asleep, while other areas are awake. The parts that are awake allow sleepwalkers to perform various physical tasks—even driving a car. Meanwhile, the asleep parts include ones that control visual recognition, so people shaken out of their slumber might not recognize the person waking them up. An episode may last a few seconds or longer than thirty minutes.

Given the dangers inherent in sleep driving or sleep cooking, experts say you should wake sleepwalkers who could hurt themselves or others. Waking them, though, might not be easy, since some areas of the brain are so deeply asleep. Pressman recommends giving sleepwalkers brief directions to return to bed.

While waking up sleep-walkers certainly won't cause any harm, arousing them from deep sleep may produce a moment of distress. At that moment, the person in danger is the one doing the waking: the sleepwalker might react with a defensive physical move, such as a punch or kick.

An engraving of the Turk from Karl Gottlieb von Windisch's 1784 book *Inanimate Reason.*

The Mechanical Chess Champion

Myth #47

"Any sufficiently advanced technology is indistinguishable from magic."

—ARTHUR C. CLARKE, science fiction writer

BELIEVE IT OR NOT, THE WORLD'S FIRST BOBBY FISCHER ATTEMPTED TO PASS HIMSELF OFF AS A MECHANICAL MARVEL. AND FOR A WHILE, HE EVEN GOT AWAY WITH IT.

One of the most famous chess masters of the eighteenth and nineteenth centuries was known as the Mechanical Turk. He bedazzled Empress Maria Theresa and Emperor Joseph II of Austria. He beat Benjamin Franklin, Napoleon Bonaparte, and several of the era's best players. But it was the clockwork nature of the Turk, not his prowess at the chessboard, that truly amazed spectators. What remains amazing today is that this artificial chess-master machine wasn't even a robot, but rather an ingenious hoax devised by a Hungarian named Wolfgang von Kempelen.

Kempelen was a tinkerer and a clerk in the Habsburg court. He was an ingenious man who invented the first synthetic voice box that could produce fully intelligible sentences, but that's not what history remembers him for. When an illusionist wowed the Habsburg court with a performance in 1770, Kempelen, unimpressed, bragged he could produce a far more remarkable spectacle. Empress Maria Theresa encouraged the clerk, and Kempelen came back months later with a robot that appeared to play chess—and win.

Of course, the Mechanical Turk was a fraud. Though this was the golden age of automatons and other clockwork spectacles, the technology of the day wasn't even capable of basic computation. In reality, the cabinet upon which the chessboard sat housed a human director, skilled at chess, who directed the Turk through internal levers and inferred the opponent's moves thanks to magnets placed underneath the board (which itself held magnetic chess pieces). The director, and by extension the Turk, played aggressively and beat some of the most gifted chess players of the era.

Many people (including Charles Babbage, the man who designed a forerunner of today's computer and who lost to the Turk) suspected all along that the Turk's engine was man rather than machine, but Kempelen's ingenuity preserved the secret for five decades. The complex clockwork innards, which the inventor showed off to both audience and opponent before each demonstration, were realistic enough to keep people from searching for and seeing the man behind the cabinet doors. The deception was so successful and complete that to deride the Turk as a hoax denies Kempelen his due: his ability to conceive of and contrive such an illusion is proof of his mastery of mechanical, as well as social, engineering.

From a book attempting to explain the illusions behind the Kempelen chess-playing automaton after the device was reconstructed.

You Can Photograph Ghosts Myth #48

For people who had lost loved ones, American photographer William Mumler's photographs offered comfort. To disbelievers, they were simply fakes. Mumler was the first known "spirit photographer," producing eerie images that seemed to miraculously include likenesses of the dead.

Mumler worked in the mid-1800s at a time when spiritualism was gaining ground in the United States. Spiritualists believe that the spirits of dead people move on to a separate realm but remain in contact with the world of the living. Mumler's photographs seemed to offer proof that the spirits were somehow still present on Earth.

Mumler was a Boston engraver with an interest in photography. A self-portrait he took revealed the faint image of a young girl behind him. At the time, photographs required glass plates to make negatives. Mumler had probably reused a plate that still had the image of the girl on it, creating a double exposure. He showed it to a spiritualist friend and joked that the girl was a dead relative. The friend accepted his explanation, and soon others came seeking portraits with their deceased family members— bringing photos of the relatives that Mumler added to his new images. Seeing a business opportunity, Mumler charged them a hefty $10 a photo. Even Mary Todd Lincoln came to his studio after her husband's assassination, and Mumler produced a picture of the presidential couple.

The otherworldly faintness of the double exposure and the sitters' willingness to believe that Mumler had photographed an actual spirit led to his success. His deception was exposed, however, when some individuals recognized other "spirits" in his images as people alive and well in Boston. Mumler moved to New York, but in 1869 was tried for fraud. At the trial, photographers explained that he used a double exposure and a trick lens to create the vague images. Although convinced Mumler was a fraud, the judge let him go for lack of evidence.

Before he died, Mumler destroyed the negatives of his work, leaving few samples of his spirited hoax.

Thomas Edison Invented a "Food Machine"

On April 1, 1878, the *New York Graphic* published an interview with Thomas Edison, describing a new food machine that could produce food and drink from water and soil.

In the interview, Edison went on the record claiming that "it will annihilate famine and pauperism." Other outlets picked up the story and the American public demanded to know when they could purchase the machine. But this invention that could change the world was too good to be true: the article was an April Fools' Day joke.

The article by the *New York Graphic* was a comment on Edison's genius that quickly escalated into a widespread hoax. Readers found the food machine article plausible because the nineteenth century was an era of major technological change. Thanks to his recent success in recording sound through the phonograph, there seemed to be no limit to what Edison might accomplish. Some sources nicknamed him "the wizard of Menlo Park," referring to the New Jersey town where he lived and worked. On April 2, the *Graphic* reprinted the original article along with embarrassing snippets from other newspapers that had failed to check their facts.

It's hard to blame the American people for buying into Edison's food machine. By the time of his death in 1931, Edison had created the stock ticker and the moving camera and made significant improvements to the telegraph, telephone, lightbulb, and electric power. His inventions changed the world, and although the food machine wasn't one of them, it reinforced his status as America's favorite genius.

We Have Only Five Senses

Musical phenomenon Stevie Wonder has been blind since birth, but he somehow learned to play the piano, harmonica, and drums, finding success at an early age. He became one of the most beloved songwriters and artists of the twentieth century, all without one of the five senses most human beings take for granted.

While Stevie undoubtedly relied on his other four senses (hearing, smell, touch, and taste), scientists say there are even more ways that we interact with the world around us than the five ways memorized by kindergartners around the globe. It all depends on how we define the word "sense."

One way of exploring these extra senses is to place a blindfold over your eyes. Note how you remain balanced—that's the fluid-filled vestibular system in your inner ear letting you know your relation to Earth via gravity. It also allows you to feel acceleration in a car and is the responsible party for seasickness on a boat.

Other senses that provide valuable info about your body include hunger, thirst, and pain. And don't forget that subtle urge for a trip to the bathroom, which becomes all the more apparent when you try to potty-train a toddler. Less obvious senses include blood pressure, blood sugar, and hormone spikes.

All of these signals provide information to our brains from the body and the outside world, expanding an accurate definition of "sense," but they rely on different receptors and could therefore fall under different categories. However you look at it, five is a pretty random number for describing your senses. Ignoring other messages from your body will leave you hungry, thirsty, tired, and needing a restroom—which is just as ill-advised as walking around with that blindfold over your eyes.

Myth #51

Homeopathy Actually Works

The late eighteenth century German doctor Samuel Hahnemann made what he considered, then, a radical medical discovery: a substance that created unhealthy symptoms in a person could, in tiny amounts, treat the same symptom if it arose from other causes.

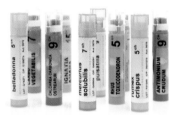

This "likes are cured by like" theory became one of the guiding principles of a new form of medicine Hahnemann called homeopathy.

Once commonly used in the United States, homeopathy is still fairly common in Europe. It's also gained a new foothold among Americans seeking alternatives to traditional Western, or allopathic, medicines. The substances used to create the minute doses prescribed in homeopathy include some

herbal remedies, which can also be taken in larger doses as supplements. As the popularity of these alternative treatments has grown, scientists have weighed in on their efficacy.

Homeopathy, most agree, is really a pseudoscience, especially since some doses prescribed actually contain none of the substance that supposedly treats a particular condition. In 2014, after analyzing previous studies on homeopathy, Australia's National Health and Medical Research

Council stated, "There is no reliable evidence that homeopathy is effective for treating health conditions." If homeopathic remedies have any positive impact, a 2005 report from the British medical journal *The Lancet* warned, it's solely because of the placebo effect.

The verdict? If you seek an alternative treatment, giving homeopathy a try likely won't hurt you. For serious illnesses, however, it's best to see a practitioner of Western medicine.

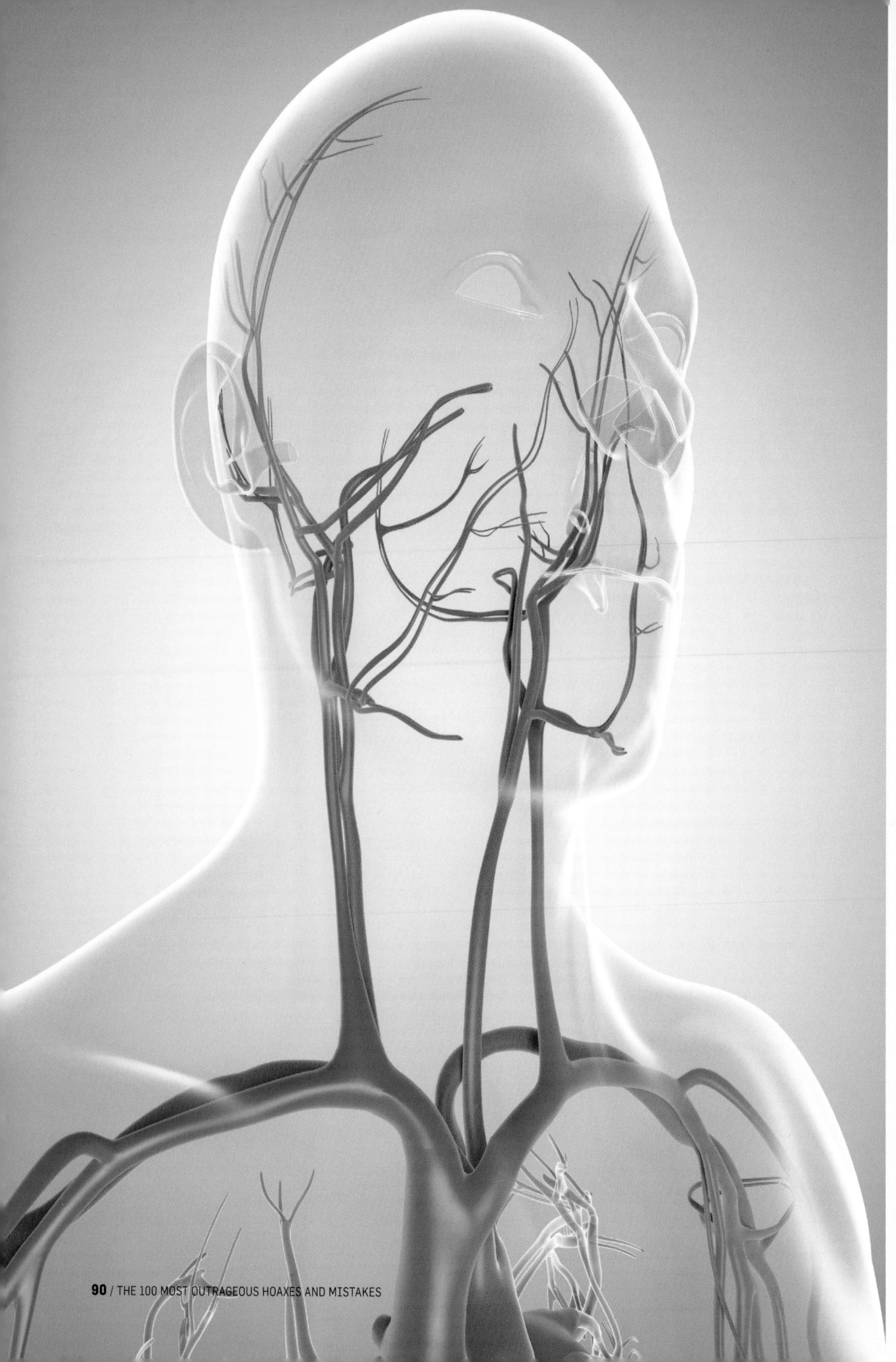

Blood Inside the Body Is Blue

Myth #52

Oxygenated blood is red, but deoxygenated blood is blue. That's why your veins are blue, right?

Wrong! Have you ever donated blood to the Red Cross or had blood drawn at a lab or doctor's office? If you had the nerve to watch the procedure, you would have noticed that your blood was a deep red, even though it was drawn from a vein into a nearly oxygen-free environment.

Your blood is red because it contains hemoglobin, an iron-rich protein in the nucleus of your red (there's that color again) blood cells responsible for transporting oxygen from your lungs to the rest of your body. Actually, the red cast of the hemoglobin protein has little to do with its iron and more to do with its nonferrous components. However, when that iron does bond to oxygen, the typically dark red hemoglobin becomes a brighter shade of red, just like any ferrous compound that rusts when exposed to oxygen.

As to why veins appear blue—well, not everyone's veins are blue. Blue veins are most obvious in Caucasians. The reason why some appear blue is due to the veins themselves, which are composed of a bluish-white material. Veins may also appear blue because the subcutaneous fat in the skin absorbs more red light from the visible spectrum, reflecting the blue light back from the skin. However, those with dark skin tones may see green or brown veins, while fair-skinned folks may see purple or dark red veins. These varying colors result from certain wavelengths reflecting off the natural pigments in the skin.

The myth of blue blood is a child of many mothers: people turning blue when they choke (though this tonal change occurs in the skin and mucus membranes, not the blood), iron turning a rusty red when exposed to air, and, not least, biology texts that paint veins blue for clarification. Nevertheless, if you're a mammal—and if you're reading this, let's assume you are— your blood is red. Want to see blue blood? Look to seafood. Lobster, crab, and clam blood is copper-laden, causing it to take on a bluish-green hue.

Animals, Real and Imagined

CHAPTER **4**

THIS SUPPOSEDLY NEW RAPTOR SPECIES TURNED OUT TO BE A MASHUP OF DINO BONES, HANDCRAFTED SPECIAL FOR THE CHINESE BLACK MARKET.

The Archaeoraptor

China's illegal fossil trade can prove lucrative to agricultural workers. Such a profit was the goal of the farmer who found several broken fossils in a shale pit, cemented them together, and sold the amalgam as an intact specimen to a fossil dealer. In 1999, the fossil made its way—illegally again, thanks to smugglers—to the United States, where it was purchased by Stephen Czerkas, an amateur fossil collector and curator of the Dinosaur Museum in Utah.

Czerkas, eager to make the fossil a key exhibit in his museum, recruited paleontologists to verify the specimen and submitted his find to three publications: *Nature, Science,* and *National Geographic.* The consulting scientists warned Czerkas that the fossil was probably a fake, doctored in China to enhance its value. *Nature* and *Science* refused to publish a paper on what the collector had named an "archaeoraptor." *National Geographic,* unaware of the paleontologists' review and the subsequent rejection by peer-reviewed journals, held a press conference and published an article on the archaeoraptor in November 1999. This proved to be an embarrassing mistake for the venerable periodical.

At no point did anyone in the professional paleontological community take the archaeoraptor seriously. Stephen Czerkas' consulting paleontologists did confirm their suspicions that the fossil combined between two and five different specimens, later identified as Microraptor zhaoianus, a small carnivorous dinosaur, and Yanornis martini, an ancient bird of prey. Nevertheless, *National Geographic*'s premature reveal immediately became fodder for creationists

who reject the very possibility of a prehistory that stretches billions of years into the past. Gleefully, some in the scientific community referred to the archaeoraptor as Piltdown Chicken, a play on the infamous Piltdown Man hoax in which British collector Charles Dawson forged a missing link between man and orangutan (see pages 32, 33).

Such glee is misdirected, however. Paleontologists have since discovered other links between birds and dinosaurs, even finding that feathered dinosaurs were common as far back as the Jurassic period. Ironically, the hoax itself obscured two great discoveries: neither *Microraptor zhaoianus* nor *Yanornis martini* was known to paleontologists before the archaeoraptor debacle. It turns out that our unknown Chinese farmer, Mr. Czerkas, and the network of smugglers in between, had in their possession not one but two remarkable fossils.

Myth #54

Humans and Dinosaurs Coexisted

Fossil skull of *Homo antecessor*—the earliest known human species in Europe.

Since the discovery of dinosaurs, many people have wondered if humans and these enormous prehistoric reptiles ever lived as contemporaries. Some creationists believe that since humans have existed since the beginning of time, they must have lived alongside the dinosaurs. But thanks to the theory of evolution, as well as data supported by fossils, scientists have largely discredited that belief. Still, the search continues for all the pieces of the evolutionary puzzle.

Support for man-dinosaur duality comes from the Bible and folklore describing dragons and ancient lizards, and even cave drawings have given credence to this theory. But according to fossil evidence, dinosaurs first appeared 230 million years ago and walked—or flew—the Earth for about 135 million years until a mass-extinction event wiped them out. But humans' ancestral line, called hominids, is much younger. One of the earliest hominid fossils, *Ardipithecus kadabba*, dates to less than six million years old. Paleontologists use a foolproof method for determining the age of fossils: relative dating accounts for the layers of rock surrounding the fossils, while radiometric dating measures the amount of radioactive decay in certain types of rock.

One glitch in this explanation? Humans are part of the primate family tree, which is much older than the hominid line. The oldest known fossils of primates trace back to 55 million years ago, about 10 million years after the dinosaurs became extinct. But some scientists, like biologist Simon Tavaré, look past fossils to find the earliest primates,

which have since separated into 200 different species. In an article published in *Nature*, Tavaré compared DNA in modern primates. From this evidence, geneticists determined that all living primates can trace their earliest ancestor to about 90 million years ago. Since the mass extinction of dinosaurs occurred 65 million years ago, this figure places primates right alongside behemoths like *Tyrannosaurus rex*.

One explanation is that evolutionary biologists and paleontologists reach different conclusions with the same data. "Our results agree broadly with a molecular estimate [and] contradict widely accepted paleontological estimates," notes Tavaré. But these early primates may have barely resembled modern humans. They may have been small, nocturnal creatures that lived in tropical forests. Tavaré even theorizes that many types of primates could have been wiped out by the same cataclysmic event. But until paleontologists discover their fossils, we have only theories—and a pretty strong certainty that man as we know him never rode the back of a *Triceratops*, as cool as it would be.

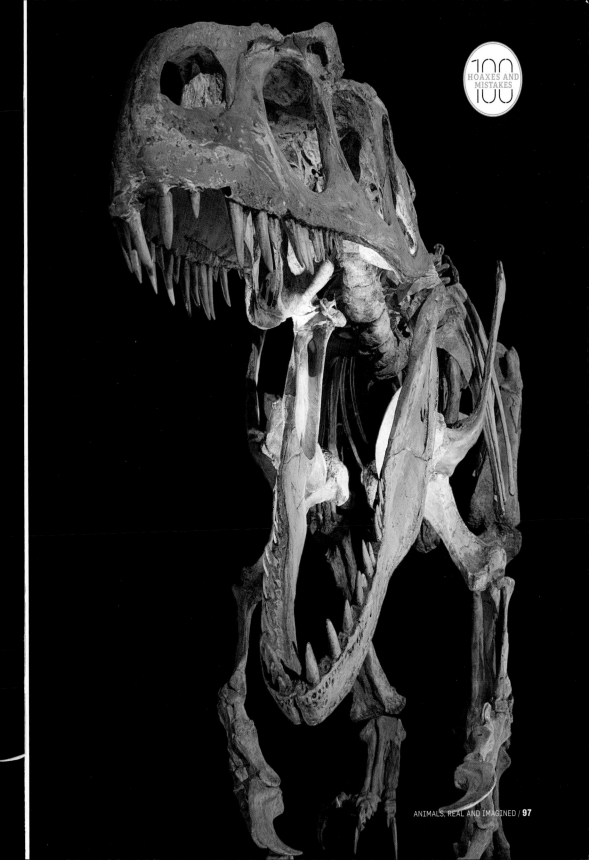

Brontosaurus Once Walked the Earth

Myth #55

Most young children grow up fascinated by dinosaurs. Vivid picture books offer colorful depictions of all sorts, including the stegosaurus, the triceratops, the terrifying *Tyrannosaurus rex*, and a pair of gigantic, leaf-eating monsters named brachiosaurus and brontosaurus.

Children memorize the names of these dinosaurs and their accompanying characteristics. The "thunder lizard" known as the brontosaurus has, in particular, captured the imagination of many children—and adults. And yet, over the past century, scientists have gone back and forth over whether it ever actually existed.

Up until recently, the paleontological consensus of most of the past century has confirmed that, to the dismay of children everywhere, "brontosaurus" is simply a synonym for a couple of species of previously discovered dinosaurs known as apatosaurus. In 1903, paleontologist Elmer Riggs argued that the anatomical differences between brontosauruses and apatosaurs were not distinct enough to classify the former as a separate genus. Since paleontologists named the apatosaurus first, the International Code of Zoological Nomenclature ruled that the alphabetically prior name also had taxonomical priority, relegating the term "brontosaurus" to junior, informal status.

Nevertheless, the "brontosaurus" moniker stuck, perhaps because museums continued to use the name in their exhibits or maybe because it rolls easier off the tongue. For whatever reason, the brontosaurus remained in the hearts of children everywhere, as well as in the scholarship of prominent paleontologist Robert Bakker, who remained convinced that *Brontosaurus parvus* and *Brontosaurus excelsus* were sufficiently distinct

to deserve their own classification.

A 2015 paper by paleontologists Emanuel Tschopp, Octávio Mateus, and Roger Benson supports Bakker's position. Their ground-breaking work employs a novel statistical approach, measuring and comparing 477 anatomical characteristics across fossil specimens to determine whether species and genera are distinct enough to warrant their own classification. Their analysis confirms what five-year-olds have long believed: the brontosaurus is indeed a dinosaur unto itself. The scientific jury is out, however, until other paleontologists replicate their work.

Bats Are Blind

Odds are you've heard or used the expression that someone is as "blind as a bat." But are bats actually blind? Science says no—all bats have sight.

In fact, some bats have better eyesight than humans, and most are roughly on par with us. In general, bats' eyes are quick to detect changing light levels. Since bats are nocturnal creatures, that ability helps them know when it's time to go out for the night.

Fruit bats, also called flying foxes, seem to stand out for their unique visual abilities. The larger of the two suborders of bats, fruit bats can see in lower levels of light than other bats, and some even see in color. Unlike most bats, fruit bats don't rely on echolocation to navigate and find food. Instead, their vision and keen sense of smell do the job. Moonlight also helps, so on moonless nights, the bats are basically grounded and go without eating.

Even for bats that rely on echolocation, vision is key for flying, as the built-in sonar system has a range of about 150 feet (45 m). A study released in 2014 showed that at least one kind of bat uses polarized light, which most mammals can't see, to help it navigate back to its nest after a night out.

Flies Live for Only a Day

Myth #57

The phrase "life's too short" is all too real for the common housefly: With only 24 hours to live, it has to soak up a lifetime of experience in less than a day. Popular folklore endorses this idea in movies such as *A Bug's Life*, but the true life span of this bug's life is not as short as you may think.

There are many types of flies—more than 120,000 species described by science and many more undiscovered varieties. Part of this rumor may stem from confusion with the mayfly, which has the shortest known life span: between 1 and 24 hours. But the common fly, *Musca domestica*, can live from 15 to 25 days. A few lucky flies even reach the geriatric age of two months.

A fly's life cycle involves four stages: egg, larva, pupa, adult. Eggs hatch into wormlike larvae that grow larger until they reach the pupal phase. From here they grow a hardened outer shell, called the puparium, and remain dormant while developing adult features like wings and legs. The mature fly ventures out to find a mate and repeat the process. The larvae-to-adult transition takes from 7 to 10 days. Without food, adults survive only two to three days. Sugar prolongs the life of an adult fly, as do cool temperatures, resulting in weeks of eating, excreting, and mating.

The common fly is common because it lives in close association with people and animals. The World Health Organization warns about the presence of flies because they transport disease-causing organisms. They congregate in excretion and waste sites and can carry diseases such as dysentery, typhoid, and eye and skin infections, so you very well might wish that these pesky insects had a shorter life span after all.

Megalodon Is Still Roaming the Seas

How big was megalodon? Imagine the shark from the movie *Jaws*, but instead of taking bites out of people or swallowing them whole, this sea monster would simply rise up and take a massive bite out of the boat.

As is the case with sharks, most of the prehistoric sea monster's skeleton was composed of cartilage, which biodegrades, thus tending not to leave behind a fossil. Megalodon's jaws and teeth, however, left behind excellent, frighteningly large fossils. Researchers estimate the size of the predator—whose name means "giant tooth"—based on the size of its teeth. Paleontologists have discovered megalodon teeth more than 6 inches (15 cm) long, implying a body size of perhaps 60 feet (18 m) long. In today's oceans, megalodon would easily dwarf the whale shark, the largest fish in the sea.

But megalodon does not swim in today's oceans. The giant predator, which first appears in the fossil record 16 million years ago, went extinct nearly three million years ago. The scientific consensus is that megalodon is no more.

Thanks to a recent work of fiction that debuted on the Discovery Channel, however-

er, there is some confusion about this matter. In 2013, the popular network opened its acclaimed Shark Week block of programming with a show titled *Megalodon: The Monster Shark Lives*. In the style of a documentary, paid actors impersonated scientists investigating fictional attacks by a fictional megalodon off the coast of South Africa. The network posted no disclaimer that copped to the bogus nature of the program, and the phony docudrama left shark biologists livid. Researchers who have a tough enough time dealing with the negative image of sharks and the harmful impact that their overfishing has on the ecosystem now have to explain to excited schoolchildren that megalodon does not exist and certainly doesn't pose a threat.

The ocean is big, and we've only explored about 5 percent of it thus far. The case of the coelacanth, a fish that paleontologists once thought went extinct more than 65 million years ago but was

rediscovered by fishermen in 1938, sparks the imagination of those who wonder what other prehistoric sea creatures we may have missed. But megalodon is not coelacanth. Megalodon was an enormous apex predator that lived in shallow waters near coastlines. A creature that big and that threatening would not—could not—go unnoticed.

REST ASSURED: THIS
MASSIVE PREDATOR HASN'T
SUNK ITS HORRIFYING
TEETH INTO ANYTHING FOR
MILLIONS OF YEARS.

Dogs Sweat Through Their Tongues

Man's best friend suffers from the heat just like humans. We sweat through sweat glands in our body, which is our way of regulating body temperature. Dogs need to do the same thing. When it's hot outside or Fido had an extra-vigorous session at the dog park, he opens his mouth and pants. Does this mean that he's sweating through his tongue?

Dogs may not have sweaty underarms, but they do, in fact, sweat. You may have spotted a trail of wet paw prints left by your dog on an especially hot day—that's because they're sweating through their foot pads, where most of their sweat glands are. Dogs are also covered by a thick layer of fur, which acts as an insulator between the hot environment and their skin. However, once a dog overheats, that fur keeps the heat from escaping, so they have to find other ways to cool off.

Panting is one of those ways. The moisture on a dog's tongue evaporates, allowing heat from the inner thorax—the hottest part of their body—to escape through evaporation from the mucous membranes on their tongue and in their mouth and throat. Sweat on humans works the same way—evaporation from the sweaty moisture on our skin lowers our body temperature. So, even though canines don't technically "sweat" through their tongues, as myth would have it, the evaporation of heat through the tongue has a similar effect.

The Flight of the Bumblebee Is a Mystery of Science

You don't need a scientist to tell you that bumblebees can fly. If you've ever seen a bee perusing the local flora in search of nectar, you observed it lightly floating from bloom to bloom, despite its bulbous body.

That said, it's not immediately obvious to the layperson *how* the bumblebee can fly. Unlike most flying creatures, its body appears much larger relative to its wingspan. Yet fly it does, and despite a persistent urban legend that science cannot explain why bumblebees can fly, their flight was never a significant puzzle of aerodynamic science.

It's true that if you attempt to model the flight of the bumblebee in the same way as that of a Boeing 747, the bumblebee would fail to remain aloft: the surface area of a bumblebee's wings cannot generate enough lift during a glide to counteract the force of gravity. But (spoiler alert) a bumblebee is not a passenger jet. By employing aerodynamic models that take into account the thrust of its flapping (i.e., not fixed or rigid) wings, researchers can and do produce solutions that predict an airworthy bee.

There are conflicting stories charting the origin of this myth, but they typically include a French or German aerodynamicist from the 1930s attempting a brief calculation of a bumblebee's capacity to stay aloft and failing to produce the expected result. This myth has generated some brilliant new research into the aerodynamics of *Bombus terrestris*. High-speed video and computer modeling indicate that bumblebees stay aloft due to the directionality of the bee's wings (more back and forth than up and down) and because the wings produce miniature vortices on their down stroke, generating lift from below as air rushes to fill the relative vacuum. This is the sort of finding that results from rational inquiry and rigorous experimentation—it's not likely to be found on the back of a cocktail napkin.

Sharks Never Get Cancer

In 1992, biochemist I. William Lane caught the world's attention with his book *Sharks Don't Get Cancer*, which claimed that shark cartilage might be able to cure cancer in humans. Since then, the idea that sharks are cancer-free has circulated widely—resulting in a bogus supplement industry that annually claims the lives of more sharks than cancer claims of humans.

It's easy to understand why this myth took off, as it is accurate that tumors in sharks are rare, and malignant ones even rarer. So far scientists have found cancer in only about two dozen of the more than 1,100 shark species. One recent discovery of tumors came in 2013, when scientists saw a great white with growths on its jaw—the first of the species known to have a tumor. And well before Lane published his book (which he eventually used to promote a shark-cartilage supplement that he sold), scientists were studying shark cartilage to see if it might have cancer-fighting properties.

Unlike humans, sharks have skeletons made up of cartilage instead of bone. Research done by Massachusetts Institute of Technology (MIT) professor and chemical engineer Robert Langer and others has shown that cartilage in general has the ability to slow the growth of tumors. Tumors require blood to grow, and they release a substance called angiogenin that stimulates the development of new blood vessels. Cartilage, and shark cartilage in particular, can prevent angiogenin from creating the new blood sources tumors need.

It's true that research has shown that shark cartilage can shrink some tumors in animals. And in one limited trial on humans, some cancerous tumors stopped growing, although they did not shrink. To most scientists, however, the limited scope of these trials and their disappointing results prove that shark cartilage is no panacea for cancer.

What distresses scientists more is that 100 million sharks are killed every year, some to make cartilage supplements that don't work—and that could keep cancer patients from using traditional treatments that do.

The Loch Ness Monster Lurks in the Deep

Myth #62

Is "Nessie" real? Legends of a creature inhabiting Scotland's Loch Ness go back almost 1,500 years. The modern tales of a monster in the lake began in 1933.

Interest in the supposed beast mushroomed after big-game hunter Marmaduke Wetherell discovered a footprint that he claimed belonged to the monster. Further

When a photo of "Nessie" taken by Robert Kenneth Wilson of London appeared in the *Daily Mail* in April 1934, many people claimed it was proof that she existed. Later study of the photograph revealed that the image had been cropped for effect.

investigation, however, proved the print a hoax—it was made with a stuffed hippopotamus foot.

London newspapers wanted photographic evidence of the sea beast, and in 1934 R. Kenneth Wilson said he had it. Wilson, a London surgeon, offered a picture of an animal with a long, curved neck topped with a fairly small head. Given the doctor's respectable profession, most people believed the photo was authentic. It took 60 years for another story to emerge: Wetherell and his son had duped Wilson into submitting a falsified photo under his name.

Between 1934 and 1994, the idea that the lake contained a sea creature, perhaps related to prehistoric reptiles, continued to attract believers and skeptics. As technology improved, scientists employed underwater cameras and sonar to try to detect a giant creature in the lake. The sonar sometimes revealed objects that Nessie believers claimed were evidence of the monster, including teeth and carcasses of sea creatures. Paleozoologist Darren Naish said most of the sonar findings and photographs could be explained by the presence of common animals, waves, or optical illusions.

In 2001, Italian scientist Luigi Piccardi suggested that small earthquakes beneath the lake could create activity on the surface that people associate with a large creature. However, not all alleged sightings corresponded with seismic activity. Whatever leads people to believe the Loch Ness Monster exists, most scientists don't buy it.

The Legend of Bigfoot

People on several continents have reported seeing large, hairy creatures—called Bigfoot, Sasquatch, abominable snowman, skunk ape, or yeti—that share characteristics of both humans and apes.

National Park. Admitting he was not an expert in digital images, Sartori found it odd that three of the four creatures disappear behind a small tree and the fourth had a strange gait, leading the scientist to believe the video was a fake. "All this makes the video quite suspect at best," he says. Most "proof" of the existence of the various hairy creatures comes not from videos but from so-called eyewitness accounts. Geologist and Bigfoot skeptic Sharon Hill notes that such testimony "is the most unreliable evidence you can have."

Seeking sounder scientific evidence for the existence of Bigfoot and related beasts, Sartori and geneticist Bryan Sykes asked people to send in hair samples they claimed came from the creatures. The scientists obtained thirty DNA samples and found

They're usually spotted in remote mountain areas, and they're typically skittish around humans, or so the reports go. Most scientists reject the idea that seemingly related, previously unknown mammals like these stalk different regions of Earth, especially since many photos and videos offered as evidence have been deemed hoaxes.

That was the verdict of zoologist Michel Sartori in 2015 after reviewing a recent video that supposedly showed a group of Bigfoots walking behind some bison at Yellowstone

that most came from familiar animals, including bears, horses, dogs, and even one human. Two samples from the Himalayas came from either a previously unknown bear species or a cross between a polar bear and a brown bear. But none of the samples pointed to the existence of the elusive Bigfoot.

Sykes admits that an unknown sample could still contain the genetic proof that Bigfoot exists. Until then, Sartori says, people can believe what they want, "but pure science only examines the proof, and currently there is none."

Duck Quacks Don't Echo

Take a noisy duck to the Grand Canyon and you may be surprised— the quack seems to have no echo. Scientists who set out to disprove this bizarre myth found that although the quack does echo, the acoustics of a duck's sounds are not exactly ready for Carnegie Hall.

Myth #64

For years, biologists and duck hunters wondered why they never heard the echo of ducks quacking, most giving a nod to the old wives' tale that duck quacks just do not produce echoes. Many children have repeated this information as fact to their friends, eager to display an expertise in most important matters.

Echoes are a delayed reflection of sound off a surface. But do ducks' quacks have some special quality that stifles the reflection? Trevor Cox, an expert in acoustics at the University of Salford in England, decided to settle the debate once and for all. His work improves the acoustics for concerts, movies, and large public spaces where speakers' voices often get muffled by the crowd (Cox uses sonic crystals—regularly spaced rods or spheres hung in a room—to diffuse echoes, thereby improving the acoustics).

After studying the sound a duck made inside an anechoic chamber (a place designed to suppress all reflections of sound), Cox then moved the duck to a reverberation chamber, designed to increase echoes. Cox noted that the quack does indeed echo, but "the sound produced is rather sinister." Cox also tested the duck's quack using virtual reality to simulate outdoor arenas, concert halls, and cliffs. All the tests turned up an echoing quack. But Cox understands why the myth exists. "Because the duck's quack is rather quiet anyway and the echo comes on the back of a fading sound field, it is as if the echo is being masked." The long "aaaacckk" at the end potentially covers up the evidence of an echo.

Frogs Won't Jump out of Boiling Water If You Heat It Slowly

Myth #65

Wrestle a frog into a pot of boiling water, and it will jump right out. But, according to one legend, if you place it in a pot of cold water and slowly turn up the heat, the frog will remain in the pot until the water boils, effectively becoming complicit in its own demise.

The myth says the frog won't notice the change in temperature until it's too late. But this tale is more of a metaphor than a recipe explaining how to cook frog, and the science to back it up is a little tough to swallow.

The story of the boiled amphibian dates back to an 1897 article in *The New Psychology* by Edward Wheeler Scripture. "A live frog can actually be boiled without a movement if the water is heated slowly enough. In one experiment, the temperature was raised at the rate of 0.0036°F (0.002 °C) per second, and the frog was found dead at the end of 2.5 hours without having moved." But the math doesn't add up. Water boils at 212°F (100°C), which means that in the span of 2.5 hours at a slow temperature increase of 0.0036°F (0.002°C) per second, the starting temperature of the water must be 180°F (82° C). At that temperature, the frog—if it wasn't already significantly injured—would surely try to leap from the pot.

Scientists also say that frog behavior doesn't support this tale. Even in cold water, these hopping reptiles don't sit still for too long, and asking a frog to sit for two hours seems pretty much out of the question. Victor Hutchison, a herpetologist at the University of Oklahoma, says all animals have a maximum temperature that they can endure, and frogs are no exception. As the water heats, the anxious frog will definitely try to escape .

Lemmings Commit Mass Suicide

Myth #66

The myth of the lemming is one of the most well-entrenched animal idioms of our culture. We're quick to invoke this misunderstood and maligned rodent whenever we believe that people are mindlessly following the crowd against their better interest.

This familiar metaphor stems from the idea that lemmings are prone to mass suicide, jumping off a cliff and into the sea, swimming off to nowhere but their collective demise.

The myth serves as a creative, if incorrect, approach to explaining a real-world mystery: Lemming populations do explode and collapse at irregular intervals. Renaissance historians explained this by claiming that lemmings generated spontaneously during rainstorms and died shortly thereafter. By the twentieth century, naturalists rejected the concept of spontaneous generation and came to believe that dramatic declines in lemming populations were due to suicidal tendencies.

The myth is on display in Disney's 1958 nature documentary, *White Wilderness*. The Academy Award–winning film depicts a colony of lemmings jumping off a cliff into the Arctic Ocean, swimming off to what the narrator implies will be their death. But the scene is entirely fake. The herd of frenetic rodents was in reality a small clutch of lemmings on a turntable, made to seem more numerous thanks to the camera's tight zoom. The lemmings did not willfully leap together into the icy sea: the producers of the film forcibly herded them off the cliff. In the end, *White Wilderness* didn't single-handedly invent the notion of the suicidal lemming, but it perpetuated the myth and granted it a wider audience than it otherwise would have enjoyed.

It's a shame, because the myth is far less interesting than the reality. Lemmings differ from other rodents in that they tend to be more aggressive toward predators. They are the only primarily Arctic rodent, and they prefer to reproduce during winter. And when they reproduce, boy, do they reproduce! Lemming populations can explode a thousandfold in a single season. After the boom, the bust is just as dramatic, with population levels plummeting to near extinction. This collapse is more mysterious, owing perhaps to infanticide by aggressive males, vulnerability to predators, or an outgrown food supply.

Before the collapse, lemmings may attempt to swim long distances—not always successfully—in search of new mates and food. It is this behavior that gave rise to the myth, but perhaps it suggests that lemmings should be a symbol of individual determination rather than collective futility.

Jackalopes Roam the West

Myth #67

It's out there, the old-timers say, a vicious critter terrorizing the wilds of the western United States. Why, they even have the evidence to prove that the jackalope, a jackrabbit with a large set of horns on its head, is real. Except, of course, it's not.

Visitors to the west may have seen postcards of jackalopes or the stuffed head of one on a wall. Doug and Ralph Herrick, amateur taxidermists from Douglas, Wyoming, created the modern version of this hybrid after a hunting expedition in 1934. They took the antlers off a deer and grafted them onto a jackrabbit that they had just killed. Then, they and others in Douglas spun a myth about the manufactured animal. Some tourists believed the tales; others realized the truth but played along anyway, bringing home jackalope souvenirs.

The Herrick brothers didn't know it at first, but rabbits with "horns" do exist, though, not like those of a jackalope. A book from seventeenth-century Europe shows an illustration of what's labeled a "horned rabbit." In the 1930s, Dr. Richard Shope learned that the horns depicted were really tumors caused by a virus. His discovery marked the first time that scientists learned a virus could cause cancer in a mammal. Today, the pathogen is called the Shope papilloma virus (SPV), and veterinarians know that it's transmitted by mosquitoes and ticks. A video that circulated on the Internet in 2013 showed a rabbit with a particularly bad outcropping of the tumors. In some cases, the horns can interfere with a rabbit's grazing and eating, causing the animal to die of starvation.

A Mother Bird Will Abandon Her Young If You Touch It

Myth #68

Perhaps you remember a time when you found a young bird out of its nest. Out of the natural compassion that comes with youth, your first instinct was to scoop up the fledgling and bring it to a grown-up for help. "No, no!" the adult said. "Leave it alone. If you touch it, the mother bird will smell you and abandon her baby."

While well intentioned, the premise of the warning is incorrect: mother birds cannot smell your scent on their young.

Actually, birds aren't very good at smelling anything. Avian olfactory nerves are notoriously simple and often cannot pick up even the strongest scents (even a skunk's discharge). If you handle a nestling or fledgling, the mother is unlikely to notice any scent you leave behind. That doesn't mean, however, that you shouldn't exercise caution. If you do come across a young bird out of the nest, it's best to contact the nearest sanctuary or avian rehabilitation facility.

So why does this myth exist, and where did it come from? Its origins are unclear, but the motivation behind it is probably the parents' desire to protect their kids (and their developing immune systems) from whatever microbes they imagine the bird harbors. Or grown-ups don't want their charges hunting for enfeebled younglings to bring into the house. Or, perhaps, the point is to keep children from doing more harm than good, a likely prospect for any inexperienced handler, let alone children not yet aware of their own strength. No matter the origin, the myth, if misleading, rightfully encourages us to exercise caution when dealing with delicate, vulnerable creatures. Not a bad idea.

Our Planet

CHAPTER **5**

Hollow-Earth Theory

Legends of a hidden world underneath our own are timeless.

From the Jewish Sheol to the Greek Hades to the Christian Hell, the concept of an underworld is a recurring trope in beliefs of the afterlife. The Buddhist legend of Shamballa tells of an ancient city beneath the surface of Earth, while the Hopi and Mandan peoples believe that their ancestors emerged from subterranean caves.

The most well-known historical figure to propose a scientifically testable hollow Earth hypothesis was the astronomer and mathematician Sir Edmond Halley. The legendary scientist who, along with Sir Isaac Newton, worked out the math and physics behind the orbits of the planets and who

first successfully predicted the return of a comet also believed that within Earth were four spheres, each surrounded by a luminous gas and likely inhabited by its own civilization. He developed this theory in 1692 to explain irregularities in compass readings, reasoning that these inner, rotating spheres possessed magnetic fields that interfered with Earth's.

Though Halley's Hollow Earth theory never caught on, the idea popped up throughout the nineteenth century. John Symmes and James McBride held fast to the idea that Earth was hollow and that the entrances to the subterranean world lie at the poles. President John Quincy Adams approved an expedition to the North Pole, but it never took place.

Today, a small group of conspiracy theorists keep the theory alive. Some tell of a sphere inside Earth that harbors another civilization. Others claim that Earth's core serves as a sun to a race of people who walk on the crust's underside. Despite claims that the government is hiding the truth, science simply doesn't back it up. The speed at which seismic waves spread is more consistent with a solid Earth than a hollow one (waves would move more slowly if they moved solely across the surface rather than straight through it). Plus, gravity tends to force massive heavy objects— like our planet— into solid balls.

Water Flushes in Opposite Directions in Different Hemispheres

Myth #70

The northern and southern hemispheres may have more than opposite seasons: Legend says that water rotates clockwise in the northern hemisphere and counterclockwise in the southern. Physics supports this theory, but the real-world effect doesn't match up.

If you stand at the North Pole and look down on the rotating Earth, you will see it turning counterclockwise. But take a trip to the South Pole and you'll see that the rotational pattern is clockwise. The Coriolis effect explains how forces in a rotating system affect mass. Water—for example, in a toilet—accelerates in the direction of the rotation. Fred W. Decker, a professor of ocean and atmospheric science at Oregon State University, says that, in reality, the direction of the water in a flushing toilet is more of an accidental twist. Local irregularities are more powerful than the Coriolis effect and the shape of the drain is likely to have much greater influence. In addition, any residual currents left over from the last time the toilet was flushed will affect the direction the water moves.

The Coriolis effect does dictate the direction of cyclones and hurricanes, which rotate in opposite directions in different hemispheres. It also plays a role in wind velocities, ocean currents, and weather patterns, thus impacting airplanes and missiles, since the distances involved are much larger than the tiny drain diameter of a sink or toilet. But unless you're using a toilet the size of a football (or rugby) field, that's another myth going down the drain.

Life Can Spontaneously Generate

Myth #71

What are the origins of life on Earth? For centuries, going back at least as far as Aristotle, some philosophers thought the answer could be found in a process called spontaneous generation in which—somehow—inanimate matter turned into living creatures.

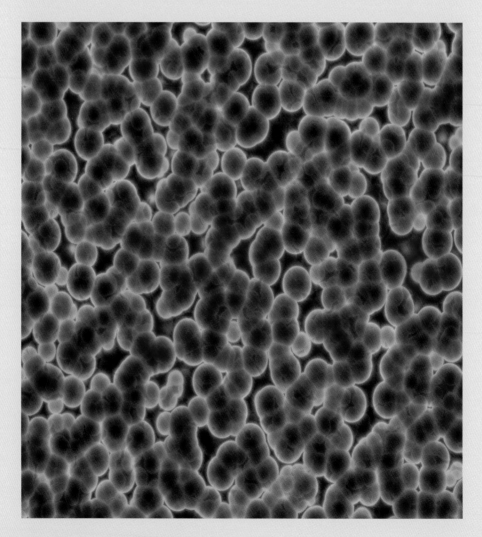

Mice were just one of the animals that early scientists suggested could be made of dead material. In the seventeenth century, Flemish scientist Jan Baptista Van Helmont wrote down a recipe that used sweaty underwear to turn wheat into the tiny rodents. (He was on more solid ground when it came to the study of gases; Van Helmont gave us the word "gas" and was the first to identify carbon dioxide and methane, among others.)

About two decades after Van Helmont's death, scientists began to test his theories. In 1668, the Italian Francesco Redi devised an experiment to disprove that maggots were spontaneously generated from rotting meat. He placed meat in open jars and in covered jars. Flies landed on the meat in the open jars and maggots soon appeared, but maggots did not develop in the sealed jars. Redi's explanation: the flies laid eggs on the meat, and the eggs developed into maggots. Despite Redi's conclusion, the scientific community continued to debate the possibility of spontaneous generation. In the early 1860s,

Louis Pasteur tried to disprove it with another experiment. He filled two flasks with boiled meat broth. One flask was shaped with a straight neck and the other with an S-shaped neck. Neither flask had a stopper. The boiling had killed any microorganisms that may have been in the broth. After several weeks, the broth in the straight-neck flask was cloudy from microorganisms entering it. The broth in the other flask was not, as microorganisms had been trapped in the bend of the neck. Pasteur concluded that the microscopic life in the first flask had come not from spontaneous generation but rather from the invisible microbes that are all around us.

Despite this experiment, the idea of spontaneous generation still sometimes comes up in debates over evolution versus creationism. But no one today disputes whether sweaty underwear will create a mouse.

An Egg Will Stand on Its End During the Vernal Equinox

It's true that you can balance an egg on its end during the vernal equinox, or first day of astronomical spring. It's also true that you can perform this feat on the autumnal equinox, the summer and winter solstices, or any other day of the year.

All you need is a bit of patience and practice, and eventually you'll be able to balance the seemingly smooth ovum, thanks to miniature imperfections across the surface of its shell. If you're as talented as the science class at Mancelona Middle School in Michigan, you might even be able to balance eggs on their narrow ends!

It's an old Chinese ritual to balance an egg during the Lichun festivals, which take place during the first two weeks of spring. These rituals are meant to bring good luck for the coming year. In 1945, *Life* correspondent Annalee Jacoby witnessed the ritual and filed a story detailing the egg-balancing ceremony. The United Press wire service picked up the story,

introducing it to papers across the United States. It is out of this piece of journalism that the modern Western myth emerged, claiming that you can balance an egg on its end during—and only during— the vernal equinox, one of two days in the year when the sun is exactly above the equator, resulting in equal hours of day and night.

Ironically, however, in China (and in most of the world), the first day of spring is *not* the vernal equinox, but rather six weeks prior to the vernal equinox; the ritual that Jacoby witnessed took place in February. In other words, the egg-balancing tradition that we imported didn't originally have anything to do with the first day of American spring or the supposed gravitational

alignment of Earth and the sun.

It is easy to debunk this myth via the scientific method. Try to balance an egg today. Try again tomorrow. Keep trying every day. Eventually you'll get good enough to balance eggs any day of the year.

Those unwilling to test this concept themselves should consider that the "science" behind the myth is nonsensical. There is no special gravitational alignment between the sun and Earth on any equinox— at any time, some location on Earth's surface will exist as a point between the sun and the center of Earth. Nor does the sun have much of a gravitational effect on a terrestrial egg; the force of your own breath is likely to exert a far stronger influence.

Lightning Never Strikes the Same Place Twice

Myth #77

This old expression was never meant to be taken as a fact of science.

The adage was intended to comfort people who had just experienced misfortune, reassuring them that they would never have to go through something awful again. But somewhere along the way, the phrase became a supposed scientific truism.

Meteorologists and storm chasers, however, assure us that lightning does indeed strike the same place twice—and often more than that. The most likely targets of multiple strikes are skyscrapers, television towers, and buildings with lightning rods. The Empire State Building, for example, is struck as many as 100 times per year. Likewise, in 2014, storm chaser Don Robinson took pictures of lightning hitting Chicago's Willis Tower (the former Sears Tower) ten times during one storm. Over several years, he's documented about fifty strikes of a single TV tower in St. Albans, Vermont.

Besides lightning often striking the same place twice (or more), one lightning bolt can actually strike two or more places. Scientists working for NASA documented this during the 1990s. Using videotape, they captured almost 400 cloud-to-ground lightning strikes. In 35 percent of these, a lightning strike hit the ground in two or more places, sometimes many yards apart.

In some cases, the lightning took multiple paths right from the base of the cloud; in others, it forked below the cloud base. Given these multiple strike points, the NASA scientists concluded that the chance of being struck by lightning is higher than the actual number of flashes.

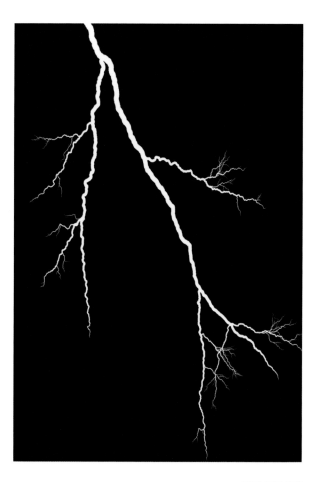

The Earth Is Flat

Myth #74

Because the horizon stretches along a linear plane as a seemingly flat expanse as far as the eye can see, it makes sense that throughout history people challenged the idea that Earth is round.

Early philosophers like Thales and Democritus believed that Earth was a short cylinder with a flat, circular top. Because our eye level sits so close to our enormous planet, we cannot see the curvature of Earth. Eventually, scientific observation was used to discover the spherical shape of our planet, but even then some people remained unconvinced.

Sometime around 500 BCE, Greek philosophers were able to use astronomy to determine Earth's shape. By observing the shadow of Earth on the Moon during a lunar eclipse, they identified our home planet as round. Aristotle famously recorded stars in Egypt that viewers could not see in northern regions, suggesting a curvature to the Earth's surface that looked out on different views of the cosmos. A century or so later, a mathematician named Eratosthenes computed Earth's circumference using simple geometry. He measured the altitude of the noonday sun at two different towns in Egypt, Syene and Alexandria. This gave him an angular difference of 7 degrees, which indicated what fraction of the way around Earth separated the two locations, conceding Earth as a sphere measuring 360 degrees. He multiplied this fraction (7/360) by the actual distance between the two towns and discovered the circumference of the Earth. Ptolemy later noted that the bottoms of mountains were obscured by the curvature of Earth in his *Almagest*—the definitive astronomy book for 1,400 years after its

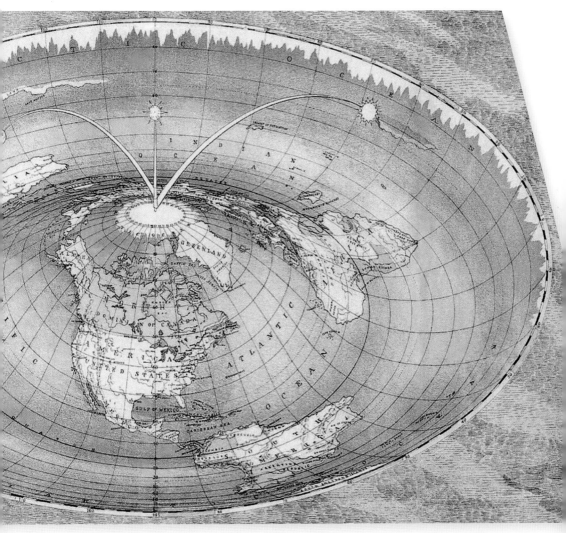

publication—and, from this era on, most educated people
took this theory as scientific fact.

In the 1520s, Ferdinand Magellan silenced the remaining skeptics when his fleet completed an unintentional circumnavigation (without Magellan, who died late en route). Today, we know from pictures of Earth taken from space that the ground beneath our feet is a sphere. While it may seem beyond basic, it took careful observations and calculations—and one adventure—to prove it beyond a doubt.

Our Planet Is Expanding

The expanding-Earth theory describes a planet that was at one time smaller in circumference and has been growing outward, causing changes in topography and other geomorphic features.

Since the time of Charles Darwin, scientists speculated that Earth's changes could indeed stem from such a large-scale process. They even applied the theory to other features like Pangaea, the supercontinent that over millions of years divided into smaller continents. But geologists now attribute Earth's changes to plate tectonics, putting the outdated expanding-Earth theory to rest for good.

Plate tectonics is the large-scale motions of Earth's outermost shell. This shell, called the lithosphere, consists of several plates that glide over the mantle, a layer of hot, dense rock. When hot material near Earth's core rises, the convection stimulates a pushing and

WHAT'S CAUSED THE CONTINENTS TO SHIFT ALL AROUND THE GLOBE OVER THE COURSE OF MILLENIA? PLATE TECTONICS—NOT AN EXPANDING PLANET, AS SOME ONCE BELIEVED.

pulling along ridges between the plates. The consequence is earthquakes and volcanoes, which create mountains and valleys. Plate tectonics also explains why the shorelines along the eastern and western edges of the Atlantic Ocean match up so nicely. At one time, Europe, Africa, and the Americas were a snug unit, but rifts now located in the ocean pushed the continents apart. Before scientists explained this process in the 1970s, an expanding Earth was one unconfirmed theory. Believers cautioned that, if true, a change in Earth's diameter could alter how we measure the planet's shape and gravity field. Processes like global warming and earthquakes would take on new meaning, and the theory could also change how we view other planets and even the origins of the universe.

Today, NASA has technology that can measure the diameter of Earth down to the width of a strand of hair. In 2011, the agency officially denied all possibility of a expanding Earth, confirming with satellites that the rate of change was statistically insignificant.

Climate Change Does Not Exist

Myth #76

In recent years, no scientific issue has generated as much heated political debate as the concept of climate change, or global warming.

Some politicians and businesses say that the evidence for climate change is not conclusive or that, at the least, any changes are not anthropogenic—caused by human activity. For some, such as Oklahoma senator James Imhofe, the idea of climate change is a hoax.

But around the world, almost all scientists—97 percent by some estimates—believe that climate change is real, and many say deforestation and the rampant burning of fossil fuels, among other causes, have increased the level of carbon dioxide (CO_2) and other greenhouse gases in our atmosphere. These gases trap heat in Earth's atmosphere.

It is true that Earth has warmed and cooled many times over the millennia. Changes in the level of solar energy reaching Earth or massive volcanic eruptions, for example, can lead to climate change. But by studying the level of carbon dioxide trapped in ice cores, scientists have determined that the level of CO_2 in the atmosphere has risen significantly since the Industrial Revolution and has spiked even more dramatically since 1950.

According to NASA, signs of global warming include an increase in ocean temperatures and record warm temperatures worldwide several times since 2005. Despite these grim statistics, some people either deny climate change is real or zero in on some points still disputed by scientists and try to use them to undermine the whole concept. Some of the deniers are scientists; others are not. But many of the deniers are on the payroll of companies that produce fossil fuels.

While debates go on in Washington, DC, and in the media, most scientists worldwide fully accept the verdict of the Intergovernmental Panel on Climate Change: "Scientific evidence for warming of the climate system is unequivocal."

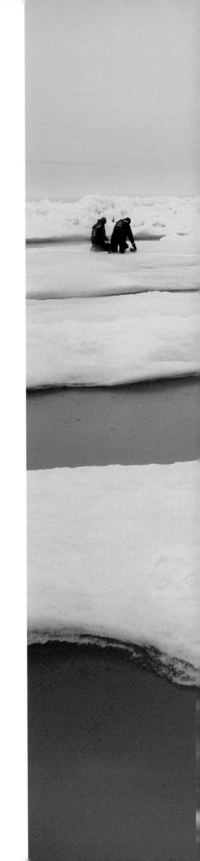

Myth #78

Chemtrails Are Poision

Look up in the sky on a clear day, and chances are you will see long, thin wisps of white trailing behind an airplane.

Some conspiracy theorists believe that chemtrails are a government plot to poison the nation, but these claims are as vaporous as the harmless condensation dissipating here.

To scientists and government officials, these wisps are harmless vapors produced by the plane's engines. But to people prone to conspiracy theories, the trails are more sinister. These so-called chemtrails, the believers say, are chemicals that harm the environment and possibly poison humans.

To scientists the white whisps are contrails—short for condensation trails. They form when the humidity is high and the temperature is low. These trails are mostly water in the form of ice crystals.

Some of the water in the trails occurs naturally in the sky. Various weather conditions determine how long the trails will remain intact and visible to the people below.

The notion of contrails actually being trails of chemicals that planes deliberately release first became popular during the late 1990s. Backers of the theory said that the US government was perhaps trying to manipulate the weather or testing chemical agents for use during wartime efforts.

The growth of the Internet helped spread the chemtrail theory, and in recent years people have posted videos purporting to show the insides of planes filled with barrels holding chemicals that produce the chemtrails.

In reality, the images showed equipment employed to simulate the weight of passengers during flight tests.

Various US government departments have tried to debunk the myth of chemtrails, though, no one denies that NASA sometimes launches rockets that release small payloads of chemicals, such as barium, that track winds in the upper atmosphere. In 2008, physicist and skeptic Dave Thomas wrote that if the government were trying to poison Americans, "What dispersal vehicle could be less effective than a craft spraying indiscriminately at 35,000 feet [10,700 m]? A low-altitude crop duster or a land truck spraying for mosquitoes would be far better at such a task." For the believers, however, denials of the chemtrails are just part of the conspiracy.

You Can "Dowse" for Water

Myth #79

For thousands of years, people called dowsers have claimed that, with the use of a forked stick or other tool, they can intuit the location of underground water.

Some say they can detect oil or gold, too. Dowsing has persisted because its practitioners seem to have some success. But what does science say?

In several controlled experiments, dowsers have not been able to find water with any significant degree of success. One German study from the 1990s did suggest that some dowsers found water more often than chance would dictate, but J. T. Enright, a physiologist and critic of that study, saw it another way. After going over all the data, he wrote in 1999, "It is difficult to imagine a set of experimental results that would represent a more persuasive *disproof* of the ability of dowsers to do what they claim. The experiments thus can and should be considered a decisive failure by the dowsers."

Scientists have suggested what might be at work when dowsers seem to find water. They might be picking up clues in the environment that indicate the presence of the liquid. And in some regions, ground water is so prevalent and close to the surface that it would be hard not to find it.

What about the vibrating of the dowser's rod, which indicates a successful find? Scientists credit this to something called the ideomotor effect. The subconscious desire to find water, or the belief that it can be found, leads the dowser to move involuntarily, causing the stick to vibrate. The ideomotor effect also explains other "supernatural" events, such as the spelling of words on a Ouija board. Science writer Michael Brooks, after his own try at dowsing and feeling the ideomotor effect, has some sympathy for people who think dowsing is real. The "illusions" that make inexplicable phenomena seem "plausible" are, he says, "astonishingly subtle and powerful."

Earth's Distance from the Sun Determines Seasons

Myth #80

Earth's slow path around the sun measures 365 days, and during that yearly trip, we experience four changing seasons on Earth. The sun is a blistering ball of hot plasma, so it makes sense to think that Earth's distance from it determines the temperature. But other factors control the reasons for the seasons, and distance from the sun isn't one of them.

It's true that Earth's orbit is not a perfect circle, but, rather, slightly elliptical, making the planet come nearer to the sun at certain times and drop farther away at other points. Common sense tells us that when a planet is closer to the radiating heat from the sun, the temperature will climb, and when it's farther away the temperature will cool off. However, Earth is closest to the sun in January (91.4 million miles [147 million km]) and farthest away in July (93.1 million miles [149.8 million km]) regardless of what hemisphere you're in. That's a difference of almost 2 million miles (3.2 million km) that has almost no effect on the turn of the seasons.

The real culprit? The slight tilt of Earth's axis. Every day, Earth spins around an imaginary pole represented by north and south. This axis doesn't stand up straight relative to the orbital plane; instead, it tilts at an angle of 23.5 degrees. Scientists believe that when Earth was young, something big knocked it slightly crooked. When the North Pole tilts toward the sun, the tilt causes an influx of direct sunlight and increased solar radiation (summer). Days are also longer, which allows more time for the sun to turn up the heat. Meanwhile, in the southern hemisphere, the rays are less direct and Earth cools. Six months later, when Earth is on the other side of its orbit around the sun, the seasons are opposite. The North Pole now tilts away from the sun and the northern hemisphere experiences winter, while the southern hemisphere enjoys the longer days and warmer temperatures of summertime.

Other planets in the solar system also experience axial tilt and seasons. Uranus has a severe tilt of ninety-seen degrees and consequently experiences drastic seasons. Venus, however, has almost no tilt and stays the same temperature all year. If Earth did not tilt at all, there would be no seasons. The temperature would vary depending on latitude but remain fairly constant all year long.

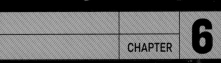

Space and Beyond

CHAPTER 6

UFOs Make Crop Circles

Crop circles were originally found in the United Kingdom in the 1970s, but the phenomenon soon spread around the globe. Intricate patterns appear in fields of wheat and other crops, seemingly popping up overnight.

Growing plant stalks are flattened in specific configurations, resulting in large-scale designs. These designs trigger surprise among locals and excitement in the press, bring tourists anxious to see a supernatural event, and tantalize theorists, who offer explanations aplenty.

With a few exceptions, most crop circles share common characteristics: the patterns are made up of circles, not triangles, squares, or any other overly complicated shapes. They form overnight and show few traces of human intervention. For decades, people have speculated about the meaning behind these very real patterns. A 1980s article in *Vogue* attributed the circles to the vigorous sexual activity of hedgehogs, but the complexity of the patterns shut that theory down. More plausible explanations involved incredibly precise wind patterns or undetectable energy fields on Earth. The most common theory, however, is that crop circles are caused by extraterrestrial aliens landing in spaceships or sending messages from faraway planets.

The circles remained a mystery until 1991, when two British men confessed that they had been planning and executing crop circles around England for two decades in an elaborate prank to make people think UFOs had landed. The men had no idea the prank would gain such momentum and provoke copycats all over the world.

While farmers are angry about disturbances to their crops, as plants are mowed or crushed to create the designs, many people admire the pranksters who take time and effort to design the patterns. The jokers are careful not to leave evidence behind, commonly accessing the crops through tramline intersections (the long, straight lines of dirt that allow farmers access to their fields). Despite the confession and plausible explanation, some conspiracy theorists still believe that crop circles may be the result of man-made weather phenomena, paranormal forces, or even shifts in Earth's magnetic field. The most tenacious conspiracy theorists still believe they are the result of extraterrestrial activity.

Geocentrism

The ancients can be forgiven for believing that Earth was the center of the universe—they had no other perspective from which to judge.

From their—and our—point of view, the Sun rose above us in the east and set in the west. The stars did the same. Better math and closer observation would prove this to be an optical illusion, but in the classical age and medieval period, geocentrism remained the dominant astronomical model.

The most enduring geocentric theory was the work of the Egyptian astronomer Ptolemy. The Ptolemaic geocentric universe imagined a static, spherical Earth at the center, orbited first by the Moon, then Mercury, then Venus, then the sun, then Mars, Jupiter, Saturn, and finally the firmament, which harbored the stars. The Ptolemaic system was remarkably successful, predicting the future locations of planets with surprising accuracy for over a millennium. Its predictive power, and the lack of a model that better explained the universe, account for its long-term acceptance.

Though there were occasional challenges, cracks really began to appear in the Ptolemaic model only when astronomers using Nicolaus Copernicus's heliocentric model of the solar system were able to produce better predictions of the future positions of the planets. Later, Galileo's discovery of four moons revolving around Jupiter—as well as better telescopic measurements indicating that the stars did in fact move relative to us as Earth orbited the sun— cemented the near-total victory of heliocentrism.

Today, a small group of biblical literalists and conspiracy theorists hold fast to geocentrism (a Gallup poll in 1999 indicated that nearly one-fifth of Americans still believe the sun revolves around Earth). If this were true, it would render everything else we know about the universe to be impossible. For example, for galaxies millions of light-years away to revolve around Earth during a period of 24 hours, those bodies would have to be moving at an incredible multiple of the speed of light—a physical impossibility. Should you wish to prove Galileo right and the doubters wrong, you need only head to your local observatory. From there, you'll clearly be able to make out the four largest moons of Jupiter orbiting the red gas giant and thus see for yourself that we're not at the center of it all.

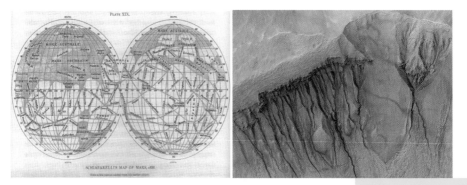

The Canals of Mars

One evening in the fall of 1877, Giovanni Schiaparelli pointed his telescope toward Mars and spied something potentially revolutionary.

Myth #83

Though the image that his telescope projected was somewhat blurry, Schiaparelli made out bright and dark features on the surface of the Mars, connected by long, straight lines that must have stretched for hundreds, even thousands, of miles. The Italian astronomer believed he was seeing a world of seas and continents, crisscrossed by a series of channels.

At the time, astronomers legitimately considered the possibility that Mars had a dense atmosphere. They knew it had a day similar in length to ours and seasons as well. If it also had water, could that mean that Mars supported life? And if Mars could sustain life,

did that mean that those channels were actually artificial creations of a Martian society?

American astronomer Percival Lowell believed so. Lowell's contention that the canals of Mars were Martian-made was so fervent that he built his own observatory in 1894 in Flagstaff, Arizona, to study Mars full time. Based on the observations at the Lowell Observatory, Lowell published three books on Mars, replete with hand-drawn maps, one specifically focusing on the canals.

Unfortunately for Schiaparelli, Lowell, and everyone else who believed in intelligent life on Mars, seeing is not

necessarily proving. As telescopes improved and more astronomers began to investigate, it became clear that not only were there no artificial canals on Mars, there weren't any canals at all. There were indeed lighter and darker areas on the Martian surface, but they were the result not of expansive seas but of variations in the reflectiveness of the planet's surface. Spectrographic readings of the Red Planet showed that there wasn't enough of an atmosphere to sustain liquid water, let alone complex life-forms.

Today, neurologists know that it's common for the brain to imagine objects in blurry pictures that aren't really there. This was almost certainly what

happened to Lowell and Schiaparelli. Worse, what the astronomers thought were canals may have been what many people see when they look at a bright object through a magnifying lens: the network of veins on the inside of the human eye. As monumental a discovery as it might have been, the canals of Mars turned out to be, quite literally for Schiaparelli and Lowell, all in their heads.

There Are Pyramids on the Moon

Myth #84

Neuroscientists have known for some time that our minds are adept at finding patterns that don't exist. This is especially true when it comes to visual processing.

Sometimes we see religious figures in the shape of a potato or piece of toast, or we see animals in a cloud formation. If you were an astronomer in the late 1800s, you might have imagined canals on Mars even though all there was to see were amorphous patches of varying brightness. If you're a conspiracy theorist in the early twenty-first century, you might see pyramids on the Moon.

Author Richard Hoagland is one such person. Since the mid-1970s, he has written extensively about extinct lunar and Martian civilizations, claiming as evidence photographs that seemingly depict artificial structures on the Moon and Mars. Unwilling to chalk his findings up to pareidolia (the tendency to see significance in random images), the amateur astronomer holds to his belief that the structures he sees are real, that the government knows they're real, and that the government is trying to keep them a secret.

One of these structures is a pyramid—Hoagland calls it a ziggurat after the ancient Mesopotamian pyramidal temples—nearly opposite Earth on the far side of the Moon. Based on "enhanced" (by whom is an open question) public images from the *Apollo 11* mission, one picture seems to show a triangular structure that Hoagland claims is more than 10 miles (16 km) high. According to Hoagland, this is one of many pyramids on the Moon which are linked to the pyramids on Earth for the purposes of deep space travel and communication.

Hoagland's claims garner no support in the scientific community. Though he has some background in science, mostly in curatorship and direction of science museums, the author holds no formal degree, has no significant university training in physics or astronomy, and has never published his work in a peer-reviewed journal.

Actual astronomers and astrophysicists, such as Stuart Robbins at the University of Colorado at Boulder and Phil Plait, former member of the Hubble space telescope team and author of *the Bad Astronomy* blog in *Slate*, have dedicated podcasts and blogs to debunking the work of enthusiasts like Hoagland. They claim that hoaxers and conspiracy theorists do far more harm than good and that—though they certainly have a right to speak their minds—the universe is a wondrous enough place without their wild fabrications.

The Atacama Alien

Myth #85

In 2003, skeletal remains found in Chile's Atacama Desert, one of the driest places on Earth, sparked a scientific mystery. The skeleton was barely 6 inches (15 cm) long and had a head that looked generally human but was abnormally sized.

To believers in UFOs and aliens, this Atacama being, nicknamed Ata, looked like the images of aliens that had filled the media in recent years. That appearance led some to see Ata as proof of alien life. In 2012, Stanford geneticist Garry Nolan tried to answer the question of Ata's origin.

Nolan did his research during the production of the documentary *Sirius*, which explores UFOs, alleged government cover-ups of these vehicles, and their extraterrestrial passengers. Even before beginning his work, Nolan knew that Ata had only 10 ribs, compared to a human being's usual 12. He showed pictures of Ata to pediatric radiologist Ralph Lachman, who said, "It didn't look, even in the pictures, like a normal human."

When Nolan finally got access to the skeleton, he ran various tests, including analysis of its DNA. The results convinced him that Ata, a male, was decidedly human, with mitochondrial DNA pinpointing his mother's homeland as most likely in Chile. The testing revealed that Ata had lived in modern times, rather than centuries ago, as some had thought. Some scientists suggested that the skeleton could have been that of a fetus, but Lachman's analysis of the data led him to think Ata had perhaps been about seven years old and suffered from an extreme form of dwarfism. He based the age on calcification in the bones. But Lachman didn't rule out that Ata was a fetus that had been naturally mummified in the extremely arid Atacama region. That process could also account for the calcification.

In 2014, Nolan said he and other scientists involved were preparing an official report of their findings. While Ata definitely raised puzzling questions, Nolan said he believed "the specimen has interesting mutations, but all mainstream genetics." In other words, the Atacama alien was anything but.

DESPITE WHAT THE POPULAR PINK FLOYD SONG WOULD HAVE YOU BELIEVE, YOU DEFINITELY WON'T BE "SEE[ING] [ANYONE] ON THE DARK SIDE OF THE MOON." THAT'S BECAUSE NO SUCH PLACE EXISTS.

The Dark Side of the Moon

100 HOAXES AND MISTAKES

Myth #86

For millennia, humans have gazed at the Moon, becoming familiar with the image in the sky but remaining ignorant about what lies beyond the view they can see. The "man in the Moon" locks his gaze down on Earth, but until recently no one had ever seen the far side.

Theories flourished about the so-called dark side of the Moon. In 1959, the Soviet spacecraft *Luna 3* transmitted the first images of the far side back to Earth. Finally, more than 50 years after those photos, scientists have an explanation for what lies beyond what we can see.

The dark side of the Moon isn't actually dark. In fact, when Earth experiences a new moon, the dark side gets plenty of sunlight. However, the "dark side of the Moon" has become a metaphor for the unknown. That far side is no longer unknown, because even though humans have never stepped foot on it, technology provides a pretty bright picture.

The side of the Moon that faces Earth consists of craters and plains called "maria" (the plural of *mare*, the Latin word for "sea"), while the surface on the hidden side is dotted with pockets and craters with fewer maria. Steinn Sigurdsson, a professor of astrophysics at Penn State University, thinks the absence of maria is due to a difference in crustal thickness between the two sides of the Moon, dating back to the beginnings of our planet.

Billions of years ago, a Mars-sized object hit Earth with a glancing blow, flinging rubble from Earth's outer layers into space. This rubble eventually formed the Moon. Early on, the Moon orbited much closer to Earth and the two bodies became tidally locked so that one side of the Moon always faced Earth. Earth was still extremely hot—more than 4,532°F (2,500°C)—and that heat radiated out to the near side of the Moon, while the other side cooled. Two elements of the rock vapor, aluminum and calcium, condensed in the atmosphere and combined with silicates to produce a thick mineral crust. Because the far side was cooler, it developed a thicker layer.

Later, when meteoroids hit the Moon, they affected the two sides of the Moon differently. On the side facing Earth, the meteoroids punched through the crust and released lakes of basaltic lava, forming the maria that make up the familiar image known as the man in the Moon. On the far side, the thick crust released no basaltic lava, instead dotting the landscape with small valleys, craters, and highlands.

SPACE AND BEYOND / **145**

Black Holes Are Actually Holes

The concept of a black hole is so abstract that many people cannot wrap their heads around it.

One common misconception is that a black hole can portal you through space: Dive into one, and you will pop out somewhere else in the universe. Or perhaps you perceive a black hole as a giant suction in the galaxy, sucking in everything around it. But even though nearby stars can "disappear" into black holes, a black hole is really not a hole at all.

Black holes are tough to study because they don't reflect light and exist extremely far away. But through observations of objects near a black hole (such as binary systems that include one normal star and one black hole), scientists have derived a vague understanding of their properties. A black hole is actually the opposite of a hole; instead, it has an enormous amount of matter stuffed into a tiny amount of space. This huge mass gives the black hole a gravitational pull so powerful that nothing can escape it, not even light. On Earth, gravity exerts pressure on us every day, but you can escape the gravitational pull of Earth by traveling 7 miles per second (11 kms). For bigger objects like the sun, the force of gravity is stronger, and an object would need to travel more than 380 miles per second (611 kms) to escape. But black holes have so much mass, and therefore so much gravity, that the escape velocity is faster than the speed of light. So even though objects and light seem to disappear into a hole, in actuality they are being pulled into a center of mass that is so big that nothing can escape.

If you by chance get pulled toward a black hole, you're doomed. But not to worry—our sun is too small to become a black hole, and we are a safe distance from other black holes in the universe.

In the northern hemisphere, you can find the North Star every night by looking for the Little Dipper. Polaris marks the end of the handle. It is the center of the clock that the northern sky ticks around, but contrary to popular belief, it is not the brightest star.

The farther north you travel, Polaris rises higher into the sky, eventually stopping overhead when you hit the North Pole. Polaris is actually a combination of three stars orbiting a common center of mass more than 430 light-years away. The primary star, Polaris A, is a supergiant about six times the mass of our sun. The other two companion stars are dwarf stars. Polaris is called a Cepheid variable because it pulsates, changing in brightness of one-tenth of a magnitude every four days or so. Considering the distance of Polaris, it has a respectable luminosity more than 2,500 times that of the sun. But there are 48 other stars in the sky that are brighter.

In this case, the most important star in the sky is not the brightest. Polaris is more accurate than a compass, but it is still not *perfectly* north. There exists 0.7 degrees of space between the northern pivot point and Polaris, less than two Moons' width. And it won't always be our North Star. As Earth's axis wobbles from the gravitational forces of the sun and Moon, Polaris will no longer indicate north. But it takes about 25,800 years for Earth's axis to complete a single wobble, so for this weekend's backpacking adventure, let Polaris be your guide.

ABOVE: Polaris, in comparison to other stars in the night sky. Below: Unlike Polaris, Sirius is so bright that it can even be seen during the day in some areas.

Alien Myth #92
Abductions

In 1966, the story of New Hampshire
residents Betty and Barney Hill
introduced the world to the idea of
alien abduction.

The Hills claimed their abduction and the
subsequent probing that they endured had
happened five years earlier. In the decades since,
hundreds of other people have claimed to have
faced a similar ordeal.

With no definitive proof that aliens even
exist, skeptics of course doubt the claim of
alien abductions, and in the years since the
Hills' experience was published, science has
offered a theory to explain why abductees
tell the stories they do.

In 2005, after conducting interviews with
about 50 abductees, Harvard psychology
professor Susan Clancy concluded that the
"victims" of alien abduction are not crazy.
Instead, they experience sleep paralysis.
Those who suffer from this phenomonen
become paralyzed during the dream state
of their sleep cycle; that paralysis prevents
dreamers from getting out of bed or
otherwise moving around as they dream.
But it's possible to wake from that state
and feel the paralysis and other sensations
many abductees say they experience. About
25 percent of all sleepers experience sleep
paralysis at some time, while perhaps
5 percent have the more extreme reactions
that could explain the memories that alleged
abductees claim are real. Clancy says, "We
can find ourselves hallucinating sights,
sounds, and bodily sensations. They seem
real, but they're actually the product of
our imagination." Sleep paralysis may also

Among UFO and alien abduction enthusiasts, Barney and
Betty Hill's story is considered
one of the most believable.

explain dreams in which the dreamers, as
they later recall, feel they can't move. Other
people who experience sleep paralysis report
waking to feel a ghostly presence in the room.

According to Clancy, another study
suggests that alleged abductees are more
likely to experience sleep paralysis than
others who don't report similar incidents.
Abductees sometimes turn to hypnosis to
understand the "truth" of their experience,
but Clancy warns that hypnosis and similar
techniques, such as guided imagery, can
actually create false memories.

Alien Autopsy

Myth #93

In 1995, millions of television viewers around the world watched black-and-white footage that claimed to show the autopsy of an alien that crash-landed near Roswell, New Mexico, in 1947.

The film supposedly proved what some believers in UFOs had claimed for decades: that the US government had gone to great lengths to cover up this first encounter with extraterrestrial life.

The film was the work of British filmmakers Ray Santilli and Gary Shoefield. They said that they had received the footage from a former US Air Force cameraman who had been involved with the investigation of the Roswell incident. When the footage appeared on TV, skeptics claimed it was a hoax. Santilli and Shoefield defended their film—at least until 2006, when a movie about the autopsy footage was about to be released, with British actors playing the two producers.

As Santilli and Shoefield now explained, and as the new movie revealed, the 1995 film was allegedly a re-creation of the original footage they had received from the soldier. It had deteriorated so badly since they had originally viewed it in 1992 that only small parts of it were visible. But that was enough for them to create a model of the "real" alien.

With the release of the 2006 feature film, Santilli and Shoefield stuck to their story that the original footage they had seen was the authentic film shot by the Air Force cameraman and had been kept a secret by the US government. Their revelation about the re-creation, though, must have embarrassed some UFOlogists who had vouched for the veracity of the original autopsy film, even as medical experts denounced it as a hoax. Few people seemed swayed by the filmmakers' later account of the alien autopsy film.

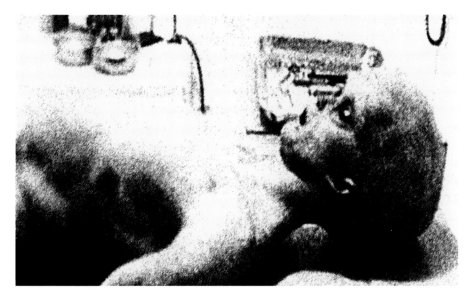

Astrology

You are probably aware of the zodiac sign that correlates with your birth date, and if you're like most people, you're skeptical about how well that sign describes you and how accurate the predictions of your horoscope are.

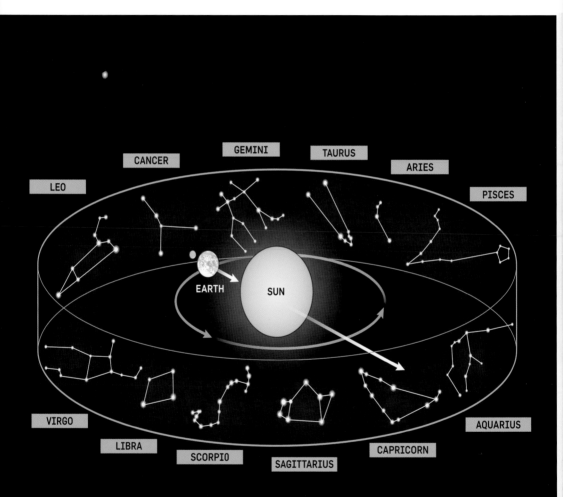

Astrologers make a living providing important financial or personal decisions based on the zodiac. Horoscopes are the medium astrologers use to make predictions based on where the constellations sat at the time of a person's birth. Heavenly bodies and star charts reinforce these astrological predictions, but for the most part, no scientific evidence for their accuracy exists.

Nearly one-third of the population in western countries believes in astrology, perhaps due to confusion with the practice of astronomy. Both words describe ways of looking at outer space and the cosmos, but they have very different applications. Astronomers measure and describe the sun, Moon, planets, and constellations, while astrologers use those heavenly objects to predict Earthly events. However, the practice of astrology predates astronomy, with origins in Mesopotamia as early as 2000 BCE. Without much understanding of the natural world, ancient people used astrology to predict the recurrence of seasons and celestial events and also to make sense of their lives. Since it took 12 lunar cycles for the sun to return to its original position, astrologers identified 12 constellations in the zodiac, each linked to the progression of the seasons. These astrologers believed in a geocentric universe in which the sun, Moon, and stars revolved around Earth. Astrology was a scholarly pursuit until the seventeenth century, when Newtonian physics and the Enlightenment dropped the guillotine on the widespread belief. However, astrology still exists today and even experienced a revival during the 1960s. Famous astrologers such as Nostradamus continue to pop up in modern folklore, renewing interest in the ancient practice.

Astrology shares a few similarities with astronomy, such as the term "zodiac," which describes the band around the sky where the sun, Moon, and planets move. But science requires systematic proof, using experiments to confirm or deny theories. In fact, as astronomers learn more about the cosmos, certain elements of astrology lose their mystique. For example, there are actually 13 signs of the zodiac. The missing Ophiuchus constellation, which in Greek means "serpent bearer" and is represented as a man holding a snake, lies northwest of the center of the Milky Way. It does not have a designated month in astrology. Additionally, astronomers say the wobble of Earth's axis means that many birth dates no longer match the traditional constellations.

Still, astrology remains significant for many: in India, you can earn a university degree in the discipline. And while many western intellectuals scoff at the idea of living life according to a horoscope, their skepticism doesn't stop them from peeking in the newspaper for advice on when to purchase a lottery ticket.

The Planet Vulcan

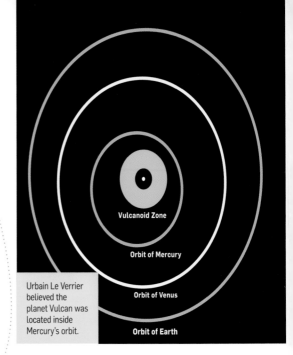

Vulcanoid Zone

Orbit of Mercury

Orbit of Venus

Orbit of Earth

Urbain Le Verrier believed the planet Vulcan was located inside Mercury's orbit.

Since Sir William Herschel discovered the planet Uranus on March 13, 1781, the question of how many planets occupy our solar system has been open.

The discovery of what was then the seventh planet, and astronomers' subsequent attempts to chart its orbit, revealed discrepancies between its predicted and actual paths that suggested another planet in the neighborhood. French mathematician Urbain Le Verrier was one of two men (the other a British astronomer) who correctly estimated the location of the eighth planet, Neptune, in 1846.

Uranus wasn't the only planet to exhibit discrepancies between its predicted and actual orbits: Mercury did as well. In an attempt to solidify his legend, Le Verrier studiously examined Mercury's orbit and predicted that there was a ninth planet, extraordinarily close to the sun, that explained Mercury's orbital inconsistency. He named the phantom planet Vulcan, after the Roman god of fire, and urged astronomers around the world to confirm its existence. A missive from an amateur astronomer in 1859 seemed to confirm Le Verrier's hunch. Physician and amateur astronomer Edmond Lescarbault claimed to have witnessed a transit of Vulcan across the surface of the sun that previous spring. This corroboration was enough for Le Verrier, for the French Academy of the Sciences, and for the French government, which awarded Le Verrier the

Legion of Honor. At that point the quest began for more data to identify Vulcan's position and orbit.

The results of this quest, however, raised doubts about the existence of Vulcan. Though data flowed in from astronomers around the world, none of the findings seemed to agree. Ultimately, some astronomers in their zeal mistook sunspots for Vulcan movement. Others claimed to see Vulcan near the sun during a solar eclipse. What they really saw were optical artifacts of the sun's light in their telescopes, or other stars not normally visible during the day.

Le Verrier died in 1877 believing he had discovered the ninth planet. But by the early twentieth century, collective doubt caused the planet Vulcan to fade from the textbooks. Einstein put the question to bed in 1915 when he proved that Mercury's orbital precession—the tendency for its orbit to shift with every revolution around the sun—was a result of the sun's relativistic effects on Mercury's local space-time.

15 years later, Clyde Tombaugh discovered Pluto, the ninth planet (for a little while, anyway).

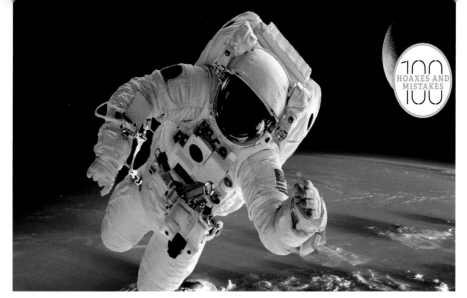

There Is No Gravity in Space

If you decide to stow away on a mission to space, be prepared for one major adjustment: weightlessness.

Myth #96

Astronauts in space appear to float in their spacecraft. An object weighing hundreds of pounds can be lifted with a pinky. Most people know this condition as "zero gravity," but the term "micro" is more accurate. Space is not the absence of gravity. In fact, gravity is everywhere. The effect diminishes with distance, but gravity from the sun, Moon, and planets is always present in space. Why, then, do astronauts float?

Earth exerts gravity on us daily by pulling us down to the surface. Gravity keeps the Moon in orbit around Earth. It holds the planets in the solar system close to the sun. It keeps the sun in place in the Milky Way galaxy. At the International Space Station, which orbits at an altitude of 200 to 250 miles (322–402 km) above Earth, astronauts live at 90 percent of gravity on Earth. That means, if you weigh 100 pounds (45 kg) on Earth, you will weigh 90 pounds (41 kg) on the space station, which is nowhere near weightless. Instead, astronauts appear to float, but they are really falling. In the vacuum of space,

where there is no atmosphere to create resistance, all objects fall at the same rate. The crew and objects fall around Earth, and since they fall together they appear to float. They fall around (not toward) Earth because the space station speeds along at 17,500 miles per hour (28,100 kmh), while Earth pulls it downward. We call the result an orbit. The same effect keeps the Moon circling Earth.

Understanding how people and equipment function in space is important for the future of the space program. Fire burns differently, crystals grow faster, and water boils in the shape of one big bubble, rather than hundreds of teeny tiny ones. Microgravity also has strange effects on the human body. Muscles and bones deteriorate and sweat doesn't drip or evaporate off skin. If humans are to venture further into space (such as the much-anticipated mission to Mars), we need to understand how microgravity will affect the astronauts, who will be away from Earth for a much longer period of time—possibly indefinitely.

The War of the Worlds

On October 30, 1938, listeners who tuned in to the CBS radio network a little after 8 p.m. heard a series of startling news bulletins: Martians had landed in New Jersey and were attacking people there.

What the listeners might not have heard, if they missed the beginning of the show, was that the story playing out on their radios was a version of H. G. Wells's novel *The War of the Worlds*, adapted by the actor and director Orson Welles.

The broadcast of the Martian invasion, it was later reported, created panic across the United States. In the days before the space program,

Director Orson Welles (right) meets with reporters in December 1938 to discuss the public reaction to his War of the Worlds broadcast.

Moon landings, and space shuttles, the only knowledge that scientists had about Mars came from their observations from Earth. Americans of 1938 might plausibly have believed that Mars had life-forms intelligent enough to build vehicles able to reach Earth. In the early part of the century, US astronomer Percival Lowell thought the lines detected on Mars' surface were canals built to transport water—a sign of intelligent life. And the great inventor Nikola Tesla once claimed to have received communications from someone or something on the red planet.

So by the time of Welles's pre-Halloween broadcast, it is easy to see why some Americans may have been deceived by the story and thought a real invasion was underway. In recent years,

however, some people have doubted that the program created the mass panic usually associated with it. Writing for the online magazine *Slate* in 2013, Jefferson Pooley and Michael J. Socolow said that a ratings service of the era found that only 2 percent of the people polled listened to the show, and CBS stations in some major markets, such as Boston, didn't even air it. The writers say newspapers created the hysteria after the broadcast as a way to suggest that radio, unlike print journalism, was not a trusted source of information. But for those who did panic, the threat from Mars seemed real enough.

The Mars-Moon Myth

Myth #98

On the Internet, everything lives forever. Embarrassing party pictures you hope your employer will never see—and astronomically absurd hoaxes. One such legend that refuses to die, despite how easy it is to debunk, is the "Mars–Moon Myth."

First circulated in August 2003, a chain letter claims that Mars is about to make an abnormally close passage near Earth. During this pass, the red planet will be so close that it will appear "as large as the full moon."

The letter continues to circulate, popping up in in-boxes every so often, usually but not always in August, with a modified date for this once-in-a-lifetime spectacle. As you might guess, it's absolute rubbish. While Earth's proximity to Mars changes as the two planets orbit the sun—Mars takes about twice as long as Earth does to complete a year—it's impossible to discern any variation in Mars' apparent size with the naked eye.

Even ignoring the implausibility of the claim, these electronic chain letters raise several red flags. First, and perhaps most obvious, is that the email keeps circulating with a new date even though nobody has yet seen Mars as big as the Moon in the night sky. Second, both Earth's and Mars' orbits are elliptical, meaning that any approach of the red planet would be gradual. If what's normally a pinpoint of light were going to transform into a disc the size of the Moon, it would be a gradual enlargement—not a sudden one that occurred on one night. Finally, although the email usually claims that the spectacle will occur alongside a full moon, the date often doesn't correspond to a full moon.

Though it would be an amazing sight, Phil Plait, author of the *Bad Astronomy* blog dedicated to debunking astronomical myths, says that Mars appears typically between $1/75$ and $1/500$ as large as the Moon. Of course, there is one foolproof way to make Mars look as big as the Moon: buy a telescope or head to your local observatory, and spy our second-nearest neighbor in all its scarlet glory.

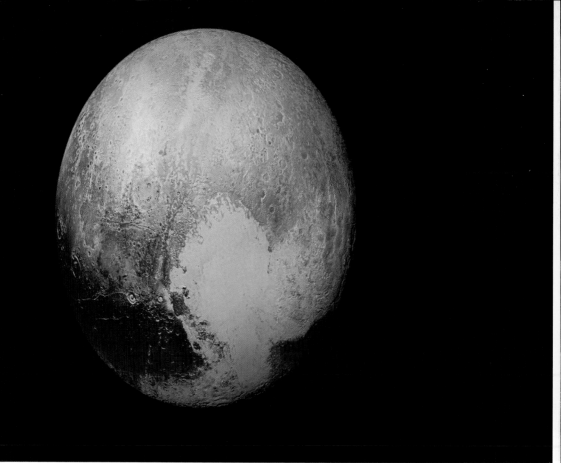

Pluto Is a Planet Myth #98

Since 1930, elementary schools around the world taught
that our solar system has nine planets, with Pluto being
the planet farthest away from the center. But in 2006,
scientists plucked the title of "planet" from the ninth rock
from the sun, leaving many students confused.

Pluto orbits the sun about 3.6 billion
miles (5.7 billion km) away, or more than
40 times the distance between the sun
and Earth. Because of that huge distance,
the diameter of Pluto remained a mystery,
although it was believed to be about half
that of Earth. In 1978, astronomers detected
a relatively large moon orbiting Pluto, whose

brightness had been mistakenly lumped with
the planet's. As a result, astronomers realized
that Pluto's diameter is 1,400 miles (2,250 km),
or about half the width of the United States.
There are seven moons in the solar system
bigger than Pluto. Even more disparaging is
the composition of Pluto, which is a tiny ball
of ice. It thus contrasts with the first four

planets in the solar system, which are made of rock, and the last four, made of gas.

Astrophysicist Neil deGrasse Tyson spoke about the necessary classification of Pluto: "If Neptune were analogized with a Chevy Impala in mass, then how big is Pluto compared to that? Pluto would be a matchbox car sitting on the curb." And, it turns out, there are many thousands of small, icy objects like Pluto orbiting past Neptune in a region called the Kuiper Belt. In 2006, astronomers found an object called Eris very similar to Pluto, but 27 percent larger. At first, scientists thought that Eris was a new planet even farther from the sun than Pluto, but the discovery prompted a debate about what makes a planet a "planet." Because Eris, like Pluto, was so far away

and so small, scientists revoked Pluto's status as a planet, instead creating a new category called dwarf planets, named because they are too small to clear other objects from their path. To date, astronomers have identified five dwarf planets: Ceres, Haumea, Pluto, Eris, and Makemake.

Scientists categorize objects in order to understand more about

them. Grouping helps astronomers understand the distinct characteristics of objects in the solar system. This may be sad news for Pluto lovers around the world, but scientists don't mourn the demotion to dwarf planet. There may be hundreds out there waiting for discovery.

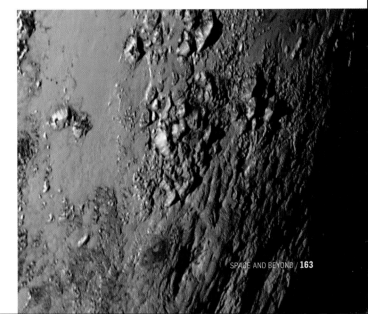

Einstein's Static Universe

Albert Einstein, creator of the theory of general relativity and perhaps the most important physicist since Newton, is responsible for his share of blunders. Einstein believed that black holes could not exist in nature (current observations suggest that they do).

He also rejected the idea of the probabilistic universe that now serves as the bedrock of quantum mechanics. However, neither of these mistakes compares to what Einstein considered his "greatest blunder."

In trying to mathematically describe the universe (using equations derived from his theory of general relativity), Einstein produced what he felt was an odd result. If his initial math was correct, the mass of the universe would cause the cosmos to curve in upon itself until it collapsed, thanks to gravity's effect on space-time. Observing that the universe did not appear to be collapsing in on itself—indeed, Einstein and many other scientists of the era believed the universe was static and eternal—the physicist introduced a fudge factor into his equations. This factor, called the cosmological

constant, mathematically counteracted gravity so that the universe would neither expand nor collapse. For the sake of convenience, Einstein imposed his assumption of a static universe on his math.

But just as Einstein was putting the final touches on his cosmological model, astronomers Edwin Hubble and Vesto Slipher were discovering that the universe was not static. Hubble used Slipher's data to show that the farther away a nebula was, the redder it appeared. Redshift is a result of luminous bodies moving away from the observer, increasing that light's wavelength, turning it red. The fact that more distant objects generally move more quickly away from us implies that the universe is not static but, rather, expanding. Upon learning of this discovery,

Einstein cursed himself. If only he had considered an expanding universe, he could have modified the cosmological constant to take this into account, perhaps even predicting Hubble's findings.

But was Einstein really wrong? Today, we know not only that the universe is expanding but that this expansion is *accelerating*. Cosmologists now attribute this finding to the mysterious dark energy that composes most of the universe itself. If the dark energy hypothesis is correct and if dark energy's pressure on the universe has been constant since the Big Bang, then essentially the cosmological constant Einstein discarded describes the effects of dark energy. Einstein may have been onto something from the beginning.

Aliens Caused the Tunguska Event

Myth #100

On June 30, 1908, a blazing fireball descended over Podkamennaya Tunguska, Siberia. Called the Tunguska Event, the blast was witnessed as far as 1,000 miles (1,600 km) away. We still lack evidence that explains the explosion, but that hasn't stopped conspiracy theorists from giving it their best shot.

In 1934, Soviet scientists surmised that the event occurred when an icy comet vaporized upon entering Earth's atmosphere, while engineer Aleksander Kasantsews declared it a nuclear explosion of possible extraterrestrial origin. American physicists proclaimed in the journal *Nature* that a small black hole collided with Earth, causing a matter-antimatter explosion. And, of course, a number of UFO conspiracy theories surfaced as well.

So what do we know about the Tunguska Event? Due to the harsh geographical and political conditions of the region, it wasn't until 1927 that Russian mineralogist, Leonid Alexejewitsch Kulik, embarked on the first expedition to uncover the mystery. He hoped to discover extraterrestrial metals and hypothesized that a meteorite had caused the blast. At the impact site, they discovered 830 square miles (2,150 sq km) of rotting timber surrounded by millions of flattened trees, many of which had been stripped of their bark and branches. Kulik and his crew were puzzled, however, when they found no sign of a crater or meteoric debris. Kulik's reasoning for the lack of meteoric evidence was that the debris sunk in the surrounding swampland, which was too soft to preserve any evidence of an impact crater.

Today, scientists posit that the Tunguska event resulted from an asteroid or a comet exploding at atmospheric pressure before reaching Earth. The blast was equal to an impact 185 times that of Hiroshima. Statistically speaking, a meteor of such size (120 feet [35 m] in diameter) is likely to strike Earth only once every 300 years; the Tunguska event is the only one for which we have firsthand accounts in the modern era.

Based on the research of Luca Gasperini at the University of Bologna in 2007, some scientists believe that a small lake in the region, Lake Cheko, may in fact be the impact crater from the fragment that caused Tunguska—mainly because there was no lake there before 1908. If extraterrestrial material were found at its bottom, it may provide solid evidence that would settle this mystery for good.

Glossary

Almagest A book by Egyptian astronomer Ptolemy, collecting ancient observations of mathematics and astronomy that were relied upon for 1,400 years before modern theories took precedence.

atom The basic and smallest unit of matter and of a chemical element.

Bigfoot Synonymous with Sasquatch, Bigfoot is a bipedal, hair-covered hominid reportedly seen around North America. Though some believe it to be fake, it is studied as a cryptid in cryptozoology.

centrifugal force The scientific term for when an object in a turning motion moves outward from the center of the turn.

cold fusion The theoretical process discovered by Stanley Pons and Martin Fleischmann in 1989 by which a low-energy nuclear reaction (LENR) is achieved, producing more energy than required. No one has since been able to replicate the original experiment or achieve definitive cold fusion.

dwarf planet A celestial body similar to a planet but too small to be classified as one by modern criteria. Pluto is defined as a dwarf planet.

Eratosthenes A mathematician who calculated a theoretical curvature of Earth a century after Aristotle suggested there was an unseen curvature to Earth. Eratosthenes's claims were confirmed by Fedinand Magellan's global circumnavigation, proving Earth is a sphere.

extraterrestrial Any object or being from, originating, or existing beyond Earth and its atmosphere. The term is often used to reference alien life, but it also describes nonliving bodies and objects in space.

Galileo Galilei An influential sixteenth-century Italian astronomer, physicist, engineer, philosopher, and mathematician, noted for his critical discoveries of heavenly bodies proving the theory of heliocentrism (in which Earth and the planets revolve around the sun as the gravitational center of our universe).

geocentrism The ancient astronomical model that portrayed heavenly bodies as revolving around Earth as the center of our universe, disproved by prevailing discoveries of heliocentrism.

greenhouse gases Gases in Earth's atmosphere (such as carbon dioxide, nitrous oxide, methane, etc.) that absorb and emit radiation harmful to Earth's ozone as part of the process of global warming. These gases are created by excessively burning fossil fuels, solid waste, trees and wood, and other materials.

Homo antecessor The scientific name for the first human species to be discovered in Europe, believed to be between 800,000 and 1.2 million years old.

The Mechanical Turk A ruse constructed by Hungarian inventor Wolfgang von Kempelen, who lived from the eighteenth to the nineteenth century, in which a fake robot above a cabinet was directed by a human director hidden beneath through internal levers. The Mechanical Turk, before being discovered, played and beat some of the world's best chess players of the era.

megalodon A prehistoric sea creature resembling modern sharks but much larger at an estimated 60 feet (18 m) long. The megalodon went extinct three million years ago.

microgravity A state of gravity being exceptionally weak, such as that experienced by astronauts in orbiting and/or traveling spacecraft. Microgravity is commonly confused with zero gravity.

Neanderthals A previous species of the Homo genus, *Homo neanderthalensis*, that went extinct. Neanderthals are the closest historical relatives to *Homo sapiens*.

neurons Cells that transmit nerve impulses, 100 billion of which reside in the human brain.

neutrinos Tiny particles with very little mass, discovered in 1959 by Fred Reines and Clyde Cowan, that interact so weakly with other particles that they can pass straight through rock.

philosopher's stone A mythical substance of alchemy, often portrayed as a stone, capable of transmuting common substances such as inexpensive metals into gold. Some also believed it to be the "life elixir," capable of bestowing immortality through rejuvenation.

phrenology A field studied by Austrian doctor Franz Joseph Gall in 1798 in which the brain was thought of as a multiorgan structure, each organ corresponding to a particular personality trait and measurable by feeling the skull above it. Though disproved for its overspecificity and lack of any foundational evidence, neuroscientists today know that certain parts of the brain do have control and influence on senses, behavior, and personality.

plasma A fourth state of matter in addition to solids, liquids, and gases. Plasma exists at a higher temperature, amorphously, expanding to fill the volume its container and is also commonly luminescent and sensitive to magnetic fields as a result of its electrons flowing free from their atoms.

spontaneous generation A theoretical process in which inanimate matter can becoming living matter, largely discredited by Louis Pasteur in the 1860s, but still the subject of much debate.

Vulcan Named for the Roman god of fire, Vulcan was believed to be the ninth planet in our solar system discovered, but it was disproved as an illusion.

Further Information

Alvarez, Walter. *A Most Improbable Journey: A Big History of Our Planet and Ourselves*. New York, NY: W. W. Norton & Company, 2017.

Brockman, John. *Know This: Today's Interesting and Important Scientific Ideas, Discoveries, and Developments*. New York, NY: Harper Perennial—HarperCollins Publishers, 2017.

Brown, Greg, and Mitchell Moffit. *AsapSCIENCE: Answers to the World's Weirdest Questions, Most Persistent Rumors, and Unexplained Phenomena*. New York, NY: Scribner—Simon and Schuster Inc., 2015.

Eaton, Gale. *A History of Ambition in 50 Hoaxes*. Thomaston, ME: Tillbury House Publishers, 2016.

Feinstein, Stephen. *Critical Perspectives on Climate Change*. (Analyzing the Issues.) New York, NY: Enslow Publishers, 2016.

Hendley, Nate. *The Big Con: Gret Hoaxes, Frauds, Grifts, and Swindles in American History*. Santa Barbara, CA: ABC-CLIO, 2016.

Nye, Bill. *Undeniable: Evolution and the Science of Creation*. New York, NY: St. Martin's Griffin, 2014.

Penrycke, Seth. *Astronomy with a Home Telescope: The Top 50 Celestial Bodies to Discover in the Night Sky*. Berkeley, CA: Zephyros Press, 2015.

Shtulman, Andrew. *Scienceblind: Why Our Intuitive Theories About the World Are So Often Wrong*. New York, NY: Basic Books—Perseus Books, LLC, 2017.

Tyson, Neil deGrasse. *Astrophyisics for People in a Hurry*. New York, NY: W. W. Norton & Company, 2017.

Websites
101 Science and Health Myths Debunked
http://www.businessinsider.com/worst-science-health-myths-2016-1/#myth-mount-everest-is-the-tallest-mountain-on-earth-38
This article from Business Insider concisely debunks 101 of the most common scientific myths, with links to articles offering more detailed explanations.

How to Debunk Falsehoods
http://www.bbc.com/future/story/20141113-the-best-way-to-debunk-myths
The BBC offers advice on the process of effectively debunking scientific myths as well as common pitfalls and how they can be avoided.

Strange But True
https://www.scientificamerican.com/section/strange-but-true/
This section of Scientific American explains unusual and counterintuitive science facts, with each article in the archive offering a detailed explanation of a particular fact.

Index

dihydrogen monoxide, 22–23
dinosaurs
   archaeoraptor, 95
   brontosaurus, 98–99
   coexistence with humans, 96
Dirac, Paul, 27
diseases
   antibacterial properties of
      silver, 59
   antibiotic use for viruses, 69
   autism-vaccine link, 56
   bloodletting, 71
   cold weather and sickness, 66
   homeopathy, 89
   leprosy, 67
   shark cartilage for cancer, 107
document 12-571-33570, 150
dogs, sweating through tongues, 104
dowsing for water, 130
drag, 14, 49
dropped penny, death by, 49
duck quack echoes, 110
dwarf planets, 162

E

Earth. *See* planet Earth
E-Cat (Energy Catalyzer), 20
echoes of duck quacks, 110
Edison, Thomas, 87
eggs, standing during vernal
   equinox, 122
Einstein, Albert, 10, 17, 164
Elizalde, Manuel, 42
Energy Catalyzer (E-Cat), 20
Enright, J.T., 130
Eratosthenes, 124
Ereditato, Antonio, 10
Eris, 162
evolution from apes, 78–79
expanding Earth theory, 126–127
expanding universe, 164

F

falling objects, acceleration of, 14
fingernail growth after death, 53
flat Earth theory, 124–125
Fleischmann, Martin, 20
Fleming, Alexander, 69
flushing water in different
   hemispheres, 119
fly life span, 101

food machine, 87
fossils, fake, 36–37, 95
France, Orgueil meteorite in, 151
frogs, heating water and, 111
fruit bats, 100
Fujimura, Shinichi, 41
Fulton, Robert, 26
fusion, cold, 20

G

Galileo Galilei, 14, 138
Gall, Franz Joseph, 54–55
Gasperini, Luca, 166
geocentrism, 138
Gibson, Lawrence, 52
global warming, 132
glucose, 53
gold, turning metals into, 12–13
Gordon, Barry, 60
gravity
   acceleration of falling objects, 14
   in outer space, 159
growing new brain cells, 72–73
gum, digesting, 64

H

Hahnemann, Samuel, 89
hair growth
   after death, 53
   effect of shaving on, 52
Halley, Edmund, Sir, 118
Hansen's disease, 67
hats, 65
head, loss of body heat through, 65
Hedland, Thomas, 42
Helicobacter pylori, 74
hemispheres, flushing water in
   different, 119
Herrick, Doug, 114
Herrick, Ralph, 114
Hill, Barney, 154
Hill, Betty, 154
Hoagland, Richard, 142
Hollander, Bernard, 55
hollow Earth, 118
homeopathy, 89
hominids, 78–79
Hoover, Richard, 151
horoscopes, 157
housefly life span, 101
Hubble, Edwin, 164

Hull, George, 34
human body
   antibiotic properties of silver, 59
   antibiotic use for viruses, 69
   aphrodisiacs, 58
   autism-vaccine link, 56
   blondes and redheads,
      disappearance of, 80
   bloodletting, 71
   cigarettes, effect on, 50–51
   cold weather and sickness, 66
   color of blood, 91
   cracking knuckles, 46
   death by falling penny, 49
   digesting gum, 64
   fingernail and hair growth after
      death, 53
   growing new brain cells, 72–73
   hyperactivity caused by sugar, 76
   leprosy, 67
   loss of body heat through head,
      65
   Mary Toft's progeny, 75
   mucus, effect of milk on, 48
   photographic memory, 60–61
   phrenology, 54–55
   right brain, left brain
      lateralization, 63
   senses, 88
   shaving, effect on hair growth, 52
   ulcers caused by stress, 74
   waking sleepwalkers, 81
humans. *See also* human body
   coexistence of dinosaurs with, 96
   evolution from apes, 78–79
Hutchison, Victor, 111
hydric acid, 22–23
hydrogen hydroxide, 22–23
hyperactivity, caused by sugar, 76

I

ideomotor effect, 130

J

jackalope, 114
Japan, Paleolithic artifacts from, 41

K

Kasantsews, Aleksander, 166
Kempelen, Wolfgang von, 82–83